VERIFIABLE EVIDENCE FOR THE BOOK OF MORMON

Also by Edward K. Watson

Is Jesus "God"? *A Witness to the World That Jesus is the Christ, the Eternal God* (in four volumes)

Ode to Jesus: *The Most Influential Person Who Ever Lived*

This is Jesus Christ: *An Interactive Aid to Understanding the Holy Bible's Core Message*

The Holy Spirit: *The God Within Us*

A Latter-day Saint Ode to Jesus: *The Most Influential Person Who Ever Lived*

The Iglesia Ni Cristo Under a Microscope: *Helping INC Members Keep More of Their Money, Survive Shunning, and Discover the Truth About Their Church and God*

Bliss: *A Guide for Women on Attracting and Keeping a Man*

Contentment: *A Guide for Couples on Maintaining a Great Companionship (forthcoming, 2023)*

The Adopted Children of God: *The Incomprehensible Fate of Christ's True Followers (forthcoming, 2023)*

10 Natural Rights: *Understanding Your Most Important Rights (forthcoming, 2024)*

How to Survive a Civilizational Collapse: *Baseline Survival Strategies (forthcoming, 2024)*

See www.edwardkwatson.com for more information.

VERIFIABLE EVIDENCE FOR THE BOOK OF MORMON

Proof of Deliberate Design Within a Dictated Book

Edward K. Watson

Brainy-Press

Copyright © 2022 by Edward K. Watson

All rights reserved. No part of this publication may be reproduced, stored in a retrieval system, or transmitted, in any form or by any means, electronic, mechanical, photocopying, recording, or otherwise, without the prior written permission of the author.

ISBN: 978-1-7779119-4-2

Cover design copyright © 2022, Edward K. Watson using Wirestock - Freepik.com File # 11342065 (Premium License). All other illustrations copyright © 2022.

Cover author photo copyright © 2022, Jeneffer M. Watson.

Distributed by IngramSpark.

www.edwardkwatson.com

Table of Contents

INTRODUCTION 1

The Unique Book of Mormon 3

What the Book of Mormon Is and Is not 6

Dictation Output 7

Two Papers 10

PART 1: ARGUMENTATIVE AND PERSUASIVE ESSAYS IN THE BOOK OF MORMON 13

Evidence #1: 2 Nephi 2 30

Evidence #2: Alma 32 47

Evidence #3: Alma 33 64

Evidence #4: Alma 34 76

Part 1: Conclusion 92

Appendix 1: Glossary 94

Appendix 2: The Book of Mormon's Structured Essays Table 97

Appendix 3: Proposed Empirical Study 106

Appendix 4: Argumentative and Persuasive Essay Tools 143

PART 2: ALMA 36'S MULTIFACETED STRUCTURE ... 145

Facet 1: Alma 36 as a Persuasive Essay 153

Facet 2: Alma 36 as a Modified Public Speech 167

Facet 3: Alma 36 as a Thematic Chiasm 180

Part 2: Conclusion 216

CONCLUSION **219**

Take the 1200-Word Alma 36 Dictation Challenge .. 220

POSTSCRIPT: JOSEPH SMITH'S SEER STONE AND INTERPRETERS **225**

BIBLIOGRAPHY **233**

INDEX **237**

List of Figures

Figure 1: Argumentative and Persuasive Essays Compared to Prose and Poetry 17

Figure 2: Argumentative Essay Structure 20

Figure 3: Persuasive Essay Structure 21

Figure 4: The Book of Mormon's Structured Essay Rhetorical Modes and Content Styles 22

Figure 5: The Scope of Jesus Christ's Atonement 40

Figure 6: The Brilliance of 2 Nephi 2:26 42

Figure 7: 2 Nephi 2's Persuasive Essay Structure 45

Figure 8: Alma 32's "Blessed" Progression and Segue Into His Prepared Essay 50

Figure 9: Alma 32's Argumentative Essay Structure 62

Figure 10: Alma 33's Argumentative Essay Structure ... 71

Figure 11: Christ's Infinite Atonement Resolves the Just and Merciful God Contradiction 81

Figure 12: Alma 34's Argumentative Essay Structure ... 90

Figure 13: Alma 36's Challenge to the World 151

Figure 14: Alma 36's Persuasion Essay Structure 166

Figure 15: Alma 36's Efficient Structure 170

Figure 16: Alma 36's Chiastic Structure Based on Primary Themes 184

Figure 17: Alma 36 Thematic Progression 185

Figure 18: Alma 36's Thematic Chiasm Using the Concentric Model 186

Figure 19: Alma 36's Chiastic Structure With Paired Unsequenced Concept Elements 207

Figure 20: Joseph Smith's Seer Stone 225

Figure 21: Artist Concept of the Interpreters 226

List of Tables

Table 1: Alma 33:22 – the Most Condensed Description of the Gospel in the Scriptures 73

Table 2: Side-by-Side Comparison of the Public Speech Version and the Personalized Version of Alma 36.. 171

Table 3: Paired and Unpaired Text Within the Alma 36 Themes 194

Table 4: Alma 36 Conceptual Pairings and Types 203

INTRODUCTION

What does a subject matter expert do when observing something they know from experience is an objective impossibility?

- A nuclear physicist witnesses a shaman transmute lead into gold.
- A biologist sees a child's toy change into a living bird.
- A medical examiner watches someone come back to life after being dead for three days.

The first reaction is disbelief – there must be a trick or fraud – some things are known to be impossible.

What if experts can examine and test this objective thing using the best equipment only to see the "miracle" repeated again and again under controlled conditions?

The worldview changes – what was thought to be a "known-known" turns out to be a "known-unknown" (we know that we do not know) or perhaps even an "unknown-unknown" (we do not know what we do not know). One's perception of reality is now suspect.

Suppose the producer of the miraculous object alleges that they created it as proof that they represent God. Wouldn't their claim become credible? Shouldn't the subject matter expert take the allegation seriously?

This is what we have with the Book of Mormon. It exists. Anyone can hold a physical copy in their hands and read it. The book claims to have been written so that the world may believe that *"Jesus is the Christ, the Eternal God"* (Title Page, 2 Nephi 26:12) and for the world to believe that the Holy Bible's teachings are true (1 Nephi 13:38-40; Mormon 7:9).

The causal logic is:

If the Book of Mormon is true, then Jesus is the Christ, the Eternal God. If the Book of Mormon is likely true, then it is likely that Jesus is the Christ, the Eternal God.

Speaking personally, my core competency is in structural linguistic semantics. I am a subject matter expert on qualitative documentation analytics and composition—the analysis, creation, and organization of complex documents—and have been doing so for more than three decades. I have created and overseen hundreds of proposals, RFP responses, project execution plans, procedures, and user manuals for dozens of clients.

What makes the Book of Mormon credible as an impossibility comparable to the abovementioned three examples? There are many, but this book only delves into my area of expertise, which includes using a Formalism-Structuralism approach to analyzing a document's:

- Internal structure – how thought modules are connected to make a larger point

- Concept development – how thought components are phrased, expanded, reinforced, and segmented

Conducting a qualitative document analysis of the Book of Mormon's internal structure and concept development shows the text's layout was purposely set. Whoever created it wrote down the text, edited it, rearranged its sentences, and rewrote it, in some places, multiple times.

The Book of Mormon's internal evidence shows deliberate design. Thought modules are coordinated, in many cases, three-dimensionally, and lack the meandering, disorganized nature of dictated writings.

Every rational book follows the same iterative creation process.

This observation is important because, unlike every other rational book, the Book of Mormon's creation was unique—it was a "dictation" process, where Joseph Smith dictated the entire text to his scribes without the aid of a written source.

The Unique Book of Mormon

Suppose when Neil Armstrong and Buzz Aldrin landed on the moon in 1969 that they discovered a book in a depression a slight distance from the Lunar Module. The book was written in English, and its cover contained a message: "This is written to convince both

4   Verifiable Evidence for the Book of Mormon

Jew and Gentile that Jesus is the Christ, the Eternal God."

They reported the discovery to the world, only to be met by skepticism and disbelief. But regardless of the mockery and dismissal, they insisted that they found the book precisely as they reported. And all evidence points to it being a genuine discovery.

Although the moon book's contents may be unexceptional compared to the millions of others on Earth, it, nonetheless, would be unique. Its existence demands a rational explanation because it should not exist. But it does. What explains it, and should its raison d'être be taken seriously?

People lose sight of what makes the Book of Mormon exceptional. Out of the millions of books in existence, it is the only one produced by a *static* dictation process.[1]

---

[1] Skousen, R. p. 4 "Witnesses of the translation said that Joseph Smith would obscure the light in the room, and, looking into the interpreters or the seer stone, would dictate the English translation to a scribe nearby. These witnesses claimed that

(1) Joseph Smith would dictate for hours in plain sight and without the use of notes or books;

(2) He would often spell out the strange names that the scribe was unable to spell; and

(3) In beginning a new dictating session, Joseph Smith did not have to be reminded of where to start."

Joseph Smith dictated the entire 269,318-word manuscript[2] to his scribes without making any substantial changes to the text after the words from his mouth were first written down.[3]

We know this not just from the eyewitness accounts but because we still have 28% of the Original Manuscript[4] (the text written by the scribes from Joseph's lips) and nearly 100% of the Printer's Manuscript (the version mainly used by the printer of the 1830 first edition).[5] They show no layout changes or resequencing. No paragraphs were inserted or moved elsewhere. No sentences were reworded or had their primary thought changed.

In short, the version of the Book of Mormon today, with its complex contents, is virtually identical to the

---

[2] Royal Skousen gave this author the 1830 Edition word count. He received it from Stanford Carmack, who used WordCruncher.

[3] Skousen, R. p. 6 "Evidence from scribal anticipations (caused by the scribe accidentally skipping ahead while writing down dictation) suggests that Joseph Smith sometimes dictated up to thirty words at a time. In general, there are very few signs of any editing or Joseph changing his mind about the translation."

[4] Ibid. p. 7.

[5] Ibid. p. 6 "For nearly one-sixth of the current Book of Mormon text (from somewhere between verses 7 and 18 in Helaman 13 to the end of Mormon), the original manuscript rather than the printer's manuscript was taken to the printer's shop and used to set the type for the 1830 edition."

version straight from the dictation process, save for non-structural changes (mostly spelling, grammar, and mechanics).

This feat may not seem like much to the non-writer, but to those with a lot of experience in structured non-prose and non-poetry writing, this *"dictated first draft is the final draft"* is an accomplishment none of us can equal. We all need to revise our first draft to correct errors and omissions and improve it. And for an uneducated 23-year-old man in 1829 to produce a 269,318-page work that did not need structural and layout enhancement on his *first* attempt at writing is something none of us can comprehend.

What the Book of Mormon Is and Is not

The Book of Mormon is not a work of creative writing. It lacks plot and character development with powerful and vivid descriptions. It lacks the rhythm and artistic beauty of elegant prose that make a reader want to continue reading. Famous books such as To Kill a Mockingbird, A Tale of Two Cities, The Color Purple, Moby-Dick, Nineteen Eighty-Four, and The Lord of the Rings are all much more enjoyable to read because they are designed to encourage the reader to keep reading them.

The Book of Mormon is utilitarian and not concerned with style or appearance. While its overall structure is narrative,⁶ its sole concern is to provide information to the reader without caring about how the text reads. Over a third of the book consists of structured essays, a ratio more common to textbooks than novels.

Dictation Output

Joseph Smith dictated the Book of Mormon while looking at his seer stone,⁷ a process that critics for two centuries have condemned to be occultic or demonic despite using objects to convey revelation and miracles is commonplace in the Bible.⁸

Observers could not see the words that Smith saw on the stone. To him, he was merely dictating the words he saw, but to observers, the words solely came from his mind. Objectively, over 500 pages of coherent, complex, and consistent text were produced from a dictation process without an observable written source.⁹

---

[6] Skousen, R. (2009). p. vii.

[7] Skousen, R. (2009). p. xii.

[8] See Genesis 44:5,15; Exodus 7:9-12; Leviticus 16:7-10; Numbers 5:12-31; Numbers 17:1-11; Numbers 26:55; Numbers 27:21; Judges 6:36-40; 1 Samuel 28:6; 2 Kings 2:14; Proverbs 16:33; Proverbs 18:18; Isaiah 6:7; Ezekiel 3:3-4; Matthew 9:20; Mark 6:13; Luke 8:44; Acts 19:11-12; James 5:14; and Acts 5:15 (!).

[9] Skousen, R. (1997).

8   Verifiable Evidence for the Book of Mormon

If Joseph Smith's dictation process occurred – as all the eyewitnesses claimed – then the Book of Mormon's contents should reflect the disordered nature of dictating ideas off the top of one's head. The book should be filled with rambling and unfinished thoughts. It should have numerous contradictions.

But it does not. Instead, it is full of organized text, with coherent thoughts and structure that can only be created by deliberate design. Most notably, it contains three-dimensional literature that can only be formed by iterative writing, where a person repeatedly re-writes text following a specific structure to enhance its effectiveness.

How can a dictated book be full of evidence showing deliberate design?

Everyone who has gone to school has experienced creating organized documents like essays and reports. Those who made three-dimensional literature like argumentative essays know that the dictation process cannot produce them.

Millions of students learn this firsthand every year – structured literature, especially those with a thesis statement, supporting argument/evidence pairs, and validating conclusion, cannot be created without study, preparation, revision, and polishing. Moreover, these complex documents need time and iterative writing. No one can produce them by following Joseph Smith's process in just a few hours; otherwise, students will be partying all night and just dictate them an hour or two before the deadline.

How did Joseph Smith do what millions know firsthand cannot be done? Not once, not twice, but 75 times?[10]

Fortunately, this subject is empirical – we can evaluate deliberate design compared to improvised production using standard analytical tools present within any university English department.[11]

Portions of the Book of Mormon, such as the 4166-word 2 Nephi 28-32, contain coherent argumentative essays. So how, exactly, does anyone, much less a young, uneducated Joseph Smith in 1829, dictate the three found in this section off the top of their head in just a day?

Those Book of Mormon passages objectively exist and cannot be ignored. If they are confirmed to be authentic structured literature, then verifiable evidence exists that the book is genuine. And if so, then the world should believe that "Jesus is the Christ, the Eternal God."

---

[10] See Part 1: Argumentative and Persuasive Essays, Appendix 2: The Book of Mormon's Structured Essays Table.

[11] See Part 1: Argumentative and Persuasive Essays, Appendix 3: Proposed Empirical Study.

10   Verifiable Evidence for the Book of Mormon

Two Papers

This book contains two papers intended for publication in academic journals but are now made available to the general public. Each paper examines evidence of deliberate design within the Book of Mormon that cannot exist in a dictated book.

The first paper, *Argumentative and Persuasive Essays in the Book of Mormon*, examines 4 of the 46 instances of this three-dimensional literature using the basic argumentative essay structure and common literary theory lenses[12] and tools (such as the primary rhetorical modes and segregated content styles). The paper examines 2 Nephi 2, Alma 32, Alma 33, and Alma 34 as empirical pieces of evidence that argumentative and persuasive essays exist in the Book of Mormon. Again, in a *dictated* work. They should not exist, but there they are.

The Alma 32-34 chapters are especially notable since their initial versions survive and can be seen in the

---

[12] This book uses Formalism/Structuralism to discern *prima facie* literary structure. Interpretation, especially on speculation of unexpressed ideas, derives from the application to the Book of Mormon text of different types of literary theory lenses, most notably, Psychoanalytical theory (to determine character motivations), New Historicism/Critical theory (for cultural, social, and economic environmental conditions), and Marxist theory (for class and production conditions).

Original Manuscript.[13] We can see that their structure in the printed Book of Mormon editions is identical to what came out of Joseph Smith's mouth. This shows the three-dimensional structure already existed when he uttered the words to Oliver Cowdery.

The second paper, *Alma 36's Multifaceted Structure*, examines the famous chapter and shows it appears to be a polished public speech that was modified for Helaman. It is structurally a persuasive essay and a thematic chiasm (not a chiasmus based on words or phrases). These three aspects of Alma 36 show it to be deliberately designed. There is no reasonable scenario where anyone could dictate Alma 36 in just the few hours it took Joseph Smith. (The reader can experience this impossibility firsthand by taking the Alma 36 challenge in this book's Conclusion.)

Like the original Alma 32-34 chapters that Joseph Smith dictated to his scribe that still survives to various extents, Alma 36 similarly survives in the Original Manuscript.[14] We know the chapter's structure was not modified after it was written down.

---

[13] Skousen, R. p. 298-307 (Alma 32), 307-311 (Alma 33), and 311-316 (Alma 34).

[14] Skousen, R. p. 319-325.

The Book of Mormon exists and demands an explanation. It is not going to go away just because it is ignored. Unless its detractors demonstrate how a dictation process can produce organized complexities like the five chapters identified in this book, it stands as actual empirical evidence for God.

And since it claims its purpose is to convince the world that Jesus is the Christ, the Eternal God and that the Holy Bible's teachings are true, if its credibility is confirmed, then so are its claims.

PART 1: ARGUMENTATIVE AND PERSUASIVE ESSAYS IN THE BOOK OF MORMON

Abstract

A dozen eyewitnesses observed Joseph Smith dictate the Book of Mormon to his scribes. Most of this occurred while he looked at his seer stone in a hat.[1] So well-known is this dictation translation process that The Church of Jesus Christ of Latter-day Saints has been condemned for it for nearly two centuries. Even the animated comedy, South Park, ridiculed the process in the episode "All About the Mormons."

Argumentative and persuasive essays such as legal briefs, patent applications, scientific papers, critical reviews, hermeneutics, apologetics, and structured debates are types of literature that require a three-dimensional logical structure to maintain coherence. They need warranted argument/evidence pairs and a conclusion that supports a thesis statement. These types of literature <u>cannot</u> be dictated outside a classroom environment within confined parameters or by someone without decades of experience in creating

---

[1] E.g., Skousen, R. (2009), p. xiii: [Emma Smith] "I frequently wrote day after day, often sitting at the table close by him, he sitting with his face buried in his hat, with the stone in it, and dictating hour after hour with nothing between us." Also, [Michael Morse] (who never joined the Church), "The mode of procedure consisted in Joseph's placing the Seer Stone in the crown of a hat, then putting his face into the hat, so as to entirely cover his face, resting his elbows upon his knees, and then dictating, word after word, while the scribe – Emma, John Whitmer, O. Cowdery, or some other, wrote it down."

> them. Everyone who has had to do them knows this firsthand. What then explains their presence in over 21% of the Book of Mormon?
>
> This paper identifies the Book of Mormon's argumentative and persuasive essays and details their characteristics. It breaks down four of these essays to demonstrate that they are valid three-dimensional structures, where the argument-evidence pairs and conclusion support a thesis statement.
>
> Given that these structured essays objectively exist in the Book of Mormon – a book that claims to have been written so that the world may believe that "Jesus is the Christ, the Eternal God," what is the most likely explanation for their presence?

Introduction

The creation of persuasive and argumentative essays,[2] especially those following the Toulmin model of argument,[3] is common in Western universities since they are proven tools to help students develop their reasoning ability. This usage stems from the need to think "three-dimensionally," whereby they must determine a thesis statement and develop logical foundations such as

---

[2] See Part 1: Argumentative and Persuasive Essays, Appendix 2: The Book of Mormon's Structured Essays Table.

[3] See Toulmin, S. E.

argument/evidence pairs and a conclusion supporting the thesis. These types of essays are architecturally distinct from prose, such as a novel, which aims to tell a story, or a newspaper article that merely conveys information. These essays' structure is also unlike poetry's lateral construction, with its façade's ordered aesthetic and rhythm. Prose and poetry do not need the logical support of a thesis statement to be successful, making them two-dimensional literature. This does not mean one is better than the other. A three-dimensional sculpture is not "better" than a two-dimensional painting; they are just different.

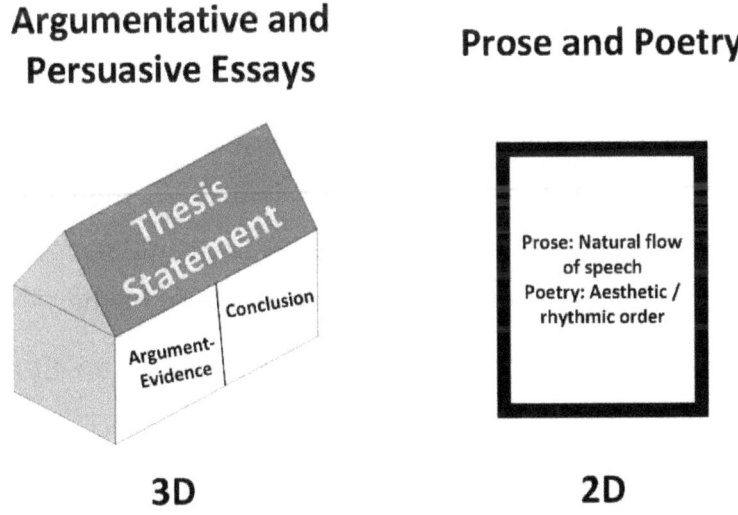

Figure 1: Argumentative and Persuasive Essays Compared to Prose and Poetry

An argumentative or persuasive essay's stylistic quality is generally irrelevant. These essays effectively convince their audience when their argument-evidence pairs and conclusion support the thesis statement using a sound warrant. Conversely, they fail when the thesis collapses from a lack of viable support. Legal briefs, patent applications, scientific papers, critical reviews, hermeneutics, apologetics, and structured debates are examples of argumentative or persuasive essays.

Just as one can be a great novelist but a mediocre poet or a legendary poet but a lousy novelist, a person can be a superb storyteller while at the same time be incapable of creating coherent argumentative essays. And the reason for this is that all forms are different types of literature. They require an understanding of their unique rules and have the literature written accordingly.

Argumentative and persuasive essays are worldview-centric – their credibility is based on what the participants accept as fact. In our case, the scientific method with modern logic, but other eras and cultures would have had different worldviews. Some examples would be the:

- Hellenistic Period: Greek cosmology with Stoic logic
- Medieval Europe: Catholic theology with Aristotelian logic
- Islamic Golden Age: Koran and Hadith with Avicenna logic

- Rabbinic Judaism: Torah and Talmud with Rabbinic logic

Assuming that the Book of Mormon people were real, they would have had their own worldview, and it would have been derived from the Brass Plates with clerical logic. This worldview would have been similar to the medieval Rabbinic Jewish practice of having their religious leaders interpret the Torah and Oral Torah on behalf of the people. The historical events detailed in the Brass Plates would have been accepted as actual events. Its mention of the coming Son of God would be sufficient to convince the people as if a deductive argument were executed.

Because the Book of Mormon people possessed a unique worldview, their reasoning process will not perfectly align with our modern Western worldview's logic, just as a Muslim with an Islamic worldview will not align with it either. Referencing authoritative religious texts like the Brass Plates or Koran to justify a belief or practice falls outside the scientific process and modern logic.

What is important from an analytical perspective is the *structure* of the Book of Mormon's reasoning process – its internal consistency and harmony with our own. Although the worldview is different, the logical process closely follows the three-part layout for argumentative and persuasive essays found in all reputable Western schools:

1. A thesis statement (the main idea, argument, or position that the author wants the audience to accept or believe),

2. the frame of argument (the body of the essay and comprises of at least one argument and one piece of evidence that supports the thesis), and

3. a conclusion (the close of the essay and contains a restatement of the thesis, a call to action, or makes the audience think or look at the world or themselves differently).

These essays can be visualized as follows:

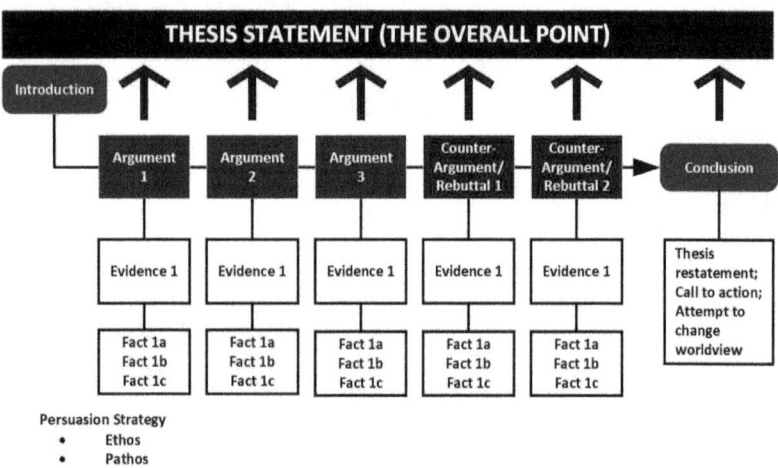

Figure 2: Argumentative Essay Structure

Part 1: Argumentative and Persuasive Essays   21

PERSUASIVE ESSAY STRUCTURE

THESIS STATEMENT (THE OVERALL POINT)

- Introduction
- Persuasion Strategy
  - Ethos
  - Pathos
  - Logos
  - Kairos
- Argument 1 → Argument 2 → Argument 3 → Conclusion
  - Evidence 1 (under each Argument)
    - Fact 1a
    - Fact 1b
    - Fact 1c
  - Conclusion:
    - Thesis restatement
    - Call to action
    - Attempt to change worldview

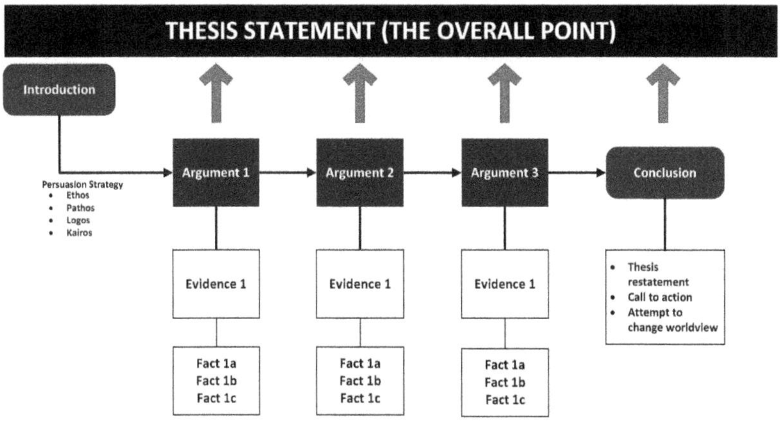

Figure 3: Persuasive Essay Structure

The argument's frame always includes at least one persuasion strategy, while the conclusion may or may not contain one.

Despite a tendency to interchange "argumentative" and "persuasive," there is a distinction between the two: the argumentative essay includes a counterargument/rebuttal while the persuasive essay does not.[4]

The argumentative essay is a more effective convincing tool than the persuasive essay since the inclusion of a counterargument/rebuttal shows the

---

[4] See Part 1: Argumentative and Persuasive Essays, Appendix 1: Glossary.

audience that potential objections were already considered and rejected.[5]

Structured Essays Within the Book of Mormon

Around 34.1% or one-third of the 269,318-word Book of Mormon (1830 Edition) is comprised of 75 structured essays of various lengths, complexities, rhetorical modes, and content styles.[6] These essays fall into one of the four traditional rhetorical modes and six content styles.

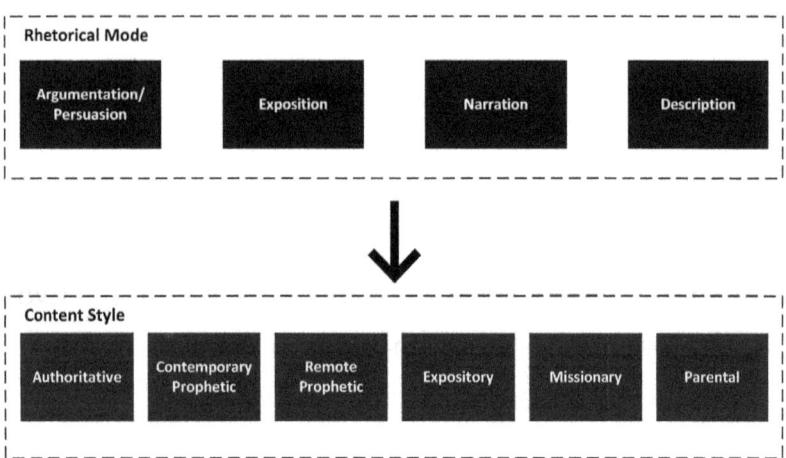

Figure 4: The Book of Mormon's Structured Essay Rhetorical Modes and Content Styles

---

[5] See Part 1: Argumentative and Persuasive Essays, Appendix 4: Argumentative and Persuasive Essay Tools.

[6] See Part 1: Argumentative and Persuasive Essays, Appendix 2: The Book of Mormon's Structured Essays Table.

Essay Structure Rhetorical Modes

All four traditional rhetorical modes[7] are found in the Book of Mormon essays:

1a. Argumentation – a composition containing a thesis statement with at least one argument-evidence pair or counterargument and conclusion that support the thesis.

1b. Persuasion – a composition containing a thesis statement with at least one argument-evidence pair in a non-counterargument form and conclusion that support the thesis.

2. Exposition – a composition structured as an instruction or lesson.

3. Narration – a composition that conveys a story without attempting to justify the essay's credibility.

4. Description – a composition that primarily uses language that allows the audience to envision or

---

[7] Although this paper separates the argumentation rhetorical mode into two (to make a distinction between argumentation and persuasion due to the counterargument variable), the author felt adopting the modern categories (Definition, Process, Cause/Effect, Comparison/Contrast, Illustration/Example, Classification/Division, Analogy) creates an unnecessary complexity to the audience. As these fit within the traditional four rhetorical modes, there is no need to be more granular given the paper's subject.

relate to the subject while not attempting to justify the essay's credibility.

Most structured essays in the Book of Mormon are argumentative essays (29), followed by persuasive essays (17), and expository essays (16).[8] Each of these requires a logical framework to maintain coherence, but the argumentative and persuasive essays require additional reinforcements to the thesis statement using argument-evidence pairs and conclusions with warrant. In contrast, expository essays merely need to avoid inconsistencies.

While 46 out of the 75 structured essays in the Book of Mormon contain the three-dimensional logical structure of argumentative and persuasive essays, other essay styles are also present. For example, the 685-word Nephi's Prayer (2 Nephi 4:16-35) and the 818-word Moroni's Sixth Essay (Moroni 2-6) are descriptive essays.[9] In comparison, the 968-word Lehi's Dream (1 Nephi 8:4-35), the 5356-word Nephi's Panoramic Vision (1 Nephi

---

[8] See Part 1: Argumentative and Persuasive Essays, Appendix 2: The Book of Mormon's Structured Essays Table.

[9] There are nine descriptive essays in the Book of Mormon. Both 2 Nephi 4:16-35 and Moroni 2-6 use an authoritative content style where Nephi and Moroni's awareness of their positions relative to their audience guided their writings. It is the self-contained structure and efficient organization of these portions of the Book of Mormon that make them essays.

11-14), and the 3758-word Olive Tree Allegory (Jacobs 5) are narrative essays. The 1442-word Nephi's Last Essay to His Brothers (1 Nephi 22:2-31) and the 872-word Nephi, the son of Helaman's Second Essay (Helaman 12), are expository essays.

These non-three-dimensional essays show signs of deliberate design, which is especially pronounced in the 1 Nephi 11-14 and Jacob 5 narrative essays due to their size and internal consistency. However, it is possible for a highly imaginative, experienced, and disciplined person to dictate Nephi's Prayer and even Lehi's Dream, given their small word count and not needing a logical structure.

Essay Content Styles

The content of the Book of Mormon's structured essays can be categorized into different styles, depending on the writer's target audience and the position of the writer relative to them. There are six distinct content styles:

1. Authoritative – the author expects the audience to obey without question because of his status or position.

2. Contemporary Prophetic – the author tells a divine message directly relevant to the writer/speaker's contemporary audience.

3. Remote Prophetic – the author tells a divine message that is primarily relevant to the reader of the Book of Mormon far in the future.

4. Expository – the author teaches doctrine so that the audience can obtain a better understanding.

5. Missionary – the author tries to convince his contemporary audience to convert or return to the true faith.

6. Parental – the author provides a loved one with a message that he believes is beneficial to the recipient.

Most of the content styles of the Book of Mormon's structured essays are expository (22), where the writer is teaching detailed and complex doctrines to his audience.

The second most common type is the authoritative (16), where the speaker or writer provides information while being in a dominant position of authority over the audience. He does not reason to convince his audience; he expects them to obey him and accept what he says as truth without question.

Interestingly, the remote prophetic styles are more numerous than the contemporary prophetic essays (16 vs.

12),[10] which supports the idea that the Book of Mormon's primary audience lives in the far future instead of during the time of the Book of Mormon authors.

The Book of Mormon essays can be tagged using the **Rhetorical Mode-Content Style** classification. For example, Samuel the Lamanite's Speech Part 1 (Helaman 13:5-39) is an Argumentation-Contemporary Prophetic essay, but his Part 2 (Helaman 14:2-31) and Part 3 (Helaman 15) are Persuasion-Contemporary Prophetic essays. Alma's first speech (Alma 5) is structurally an Argumentation-Missionary, but his second speech (Alma 7) is a Persuasion-Missionary. Alma's Ninth Essay (Alma 36) is a Persuasion-Expository, but his Fifteenth Essay (Alma 42) is an Argumentation-Expository.

The **Exposition-Authoritative** essay is the most dominant of all the essays, where information is given within a rhetorical mode and content style that conveys absolute dominance over the audience. Interestingly, the only Book of Mormon author to use the Exposition-

---

[10] The 5356-word Nephi's Panoramic Vision essay (1 Nephi 11-14) and the 879-word Jacob's First Essay (2 Nephi 6:2-18) start as contemporary prophetic styles but segue into remote prophetic essays (which this paper assigns a half-count for each within a single essay). The first half of the visions were directly relevant to those who heard Nephi and Jacob's voices in the 6th century BC, while the second half is primarily relevant to people today.

Authoritative model was Jesus Christ in 3 Nephi and Ether. Seven of the eight essays he gave followed this format.[11]

This paper focuses on the presence of argumentative and persuasive essays within the Book of Mormon[12] since no one who has done them can credibly assert they can create them off the top of their head in a few hours. The specific logical structure of these essays can only be made from deliberate design. What are they doing in a known dictated book?[13]

No credible lawyer without decades of experience will claim he can create a legal brief for a critical case in a few

---

[11] See 3 Nephi 11:22-41; 3 Nephi 12-14; 3 Nephi 15:3-10,12-16:20; 3 Nephi 18:5-7,10-16,18-25,27-35; 3 Nephi 20:10-23:5; 3 Nephi 27:4-33; Ether 4:6-19. Only Christ's descriptive essay in 3 Nephi 9:2-22, 10:4-7 deviates from this pattern.

[12] This author's philosophy is to write to the nonspecialist. Consequently, the Book of Mormon text used within this paper is the 1981 edition instead of the 1830 edition or the critical text.

[13] There were a dozen eyewitnesses who observed Joseph Smith dictate the Book of Mormon while he was looking at his seer stone (Emma Smith, Martin Harris, Oliver Cowdery, Elizabeth Ann Whitmer Cowdery, David Whitmer, William Smith, Lucy Mack Smith, Michael Morse, Sarah Hellor Conrad, Isaac Hale, Reuben Hale, and Joseph Knight Sr.) per Maxwell, N. A. Not one of them ever claimed he read from any other source material during the dictation process.

hours or days by merely dictating it without revising afterward. No scientist will claim likewise when making a scientific paper. But Joseph Smith could dictate these types of argumentative essays. Subject matter experts know this process is impossible[14] – how did he do it? Even more impressive, who today could dictate these types of essays following the "dictated first draft is the final draft" process, where they cannot structurally revise the documents after dictation?

The Book of Mormon was created in 1829, well before Stephen Toulmin published his *The Uses of Argument* in 1958, which identified the proper layout of a compelling argument. And while Samuel Newman's book on the principle and rules of rhetoric was published a few years prior in 1827,[15] it is unlikely a person like Joseph Smith could have absorbed that dense book in such a way to make the mental leap to create 75 structured essays in the Book of Mormon containing all four primary rhetorical modes. And it still does not explain how he could dictate them.

---

[14] It is easy to demonstrate this. **Take the 1200-Word Alma 36 Dictation Challenge** in this book's conclusion. A measly two-hour effort is all that is needed to empirically prove that Joseph Smith did the impossible.

[15] See Newman, S. P.

If just one argumentative or persuasive essay is valid within the Book of Mormon, then verifiable evidence exists that an apparent impossibility occurs within a dictated book. But, as this paper will show with four examples, there is more than one instance of apparent impossibilities within the book – and they are not confirmation bias fallacies.

And the reason why this can be asserted with confidence is that we *know* how to create argumentative and persuasive essays – millions of people produce them every year. And each one knows from firsthand experience that it is highly implausible that they can make them by merely dictating them.

This recognition poses an immense challenge to those who reject the Book of Mormon:

> *What explains the presence of argumentative and persuasive essays within a known "dictated" book that claims it was written so that people may believe that "Jesus is the Christ, the Eternal God" (Title Page) and that the Holy Bible's teachings are true (1 Nephi 13:38-40; Mormon 7:8-9)?*

Evidence #1: 2 Nephi 2

Essay Classification: Persuasion-Expository

2 Nephi 2 is part of Lehi's final teachings to his people as he's about to die. This chapter is the second of three

essays and is an intellectual tour de force of a lifetime of thought on big and profound ideas concerning God and humanity. Lehi passes this information onto his son, Jacob, who will inherit his father's prophetic mantle after Nephi becomes king (2 Nephi 6:2-3). Jacob's coming role as the "theologian" over the people is why the essay is structurally a persuasion instead of an exposition. This is so that Jacob can use the composition to convince his people since he, himself, did not need swaying, given that he was one of those who saw the coming Savior in a vision (2 Nephi 2:3-4; 11:3).

Jacob's vision confirms the truthfulness of Lehi's essay, which makes his experience the evaluation criterion of the composition. To say it another way, Jacob uses what he knows he knows (his "known-known") to judge his father's teaching.

Lehi uses five paraenesis or exhortative arguments to encourage his people to continue transitioning off the Law-centered salvation model they inherited from traditional Judaism to a Messiah-centered salvation worldview. They are all written in the expository style.

Thesis Position
No one can be justified or saved by the law (v. 5).

Lehi's thesis or primary point is that no one can be justified or saved by the law. This view, most prominent with Paul in the New Testament, is because the law requires punishment for every offense. And since we have all sinned due to Adam's Fall, none of us can be saved according to the law.

As people who were still practicing the Law of Moses, it appears likely that the inertia of practicing the Jewish observances and rituals led to confusion or outright rejection of the Messiah-centered model by some members of the group (perhaps by Ishmael's sons who were incorporated into the tribe under Lehi's leadership).

Frame of Argument

Argument 1

Redemption can only come in and through the Holy Messiah (v. 6).

After pointing out that men are cut off by the law and become miserable forever, Lehi declares that our redemption from the consequences of breaking the law comes from the Holy Messiah.

Evidence 1

[The Holy Messiah] offereth himself a sacrifice for sin, to answer the ends of the law, unto all those who have a broken heart and a contrite spirit; and unto none else can the ends of the law be answered (v. 7).

Persuasion Strategy	Argument Type	Evidence Type
Ethos	Deduction	Objective

Lehi uses an Ethos persuasion strategy because he's speaking as the "sheik" of his tribe whose word is the law and as one who has seen the coming Savior in a vision. The argument is stated as a fact, and the evidence is objective since it is based on a shared experience between Lehi, Jacob, and even Nephi, where all three saw the coming of the Son of God (1 Nephi 1:8; 10:17; 11:3,7,20-21,27-34; 2 Nephi 2:3-4).[16] Each can corroborate what the other is saying.

Argument 2

No flesh can dwell in the presence of God, save it be through the merits, and mercy, and grace of the Holy Messiah (v. 8).

Lehi claims the Holy Messiah is the gatekeeper to God.

Evidence 1

[The Holy Messiah] layeth down his life according to the flesh, and taketh it again by the power of the Spirit, that he may bring

---

[16] This paper considers evidence to be "objective" when multiple eyewitnesses reported that they saw the same thing, despite the experience being individually subjective.

to pass the resurrection of the dead, being the first that should rise.

Persuasion Strategy	Argument Type	Evidence Type
Ethos	Deduction	Objective

Lehi provides a deductive argument because the recipient, Jacob, knows firsthand from his own vision that this is true. This is objective and not subjective because multiple people saw the same vision.

Evidence 2

[The Holy Messiah] shall make intercession for all the children of men; and they that believe in him shall be saved. And because of the intercession for all, all men come unto God; wherefore, they stand in the presence of him, to be judged of him according to the truth and holiness which is in him (v. 9-10).

Lehi claims the Holy Messiah creates the mediation between God and all humans as the explanation for the teaching that all, both the good and the bad, will stand before God one day to be judged. Were it not for the Messiah's intercession, we cannot stand before God for judgment.

Persuasion Strategy	Argument Type	Evidence Type
Ethos	Deduction	Objective

The evidence is deductive and objective because Jacob knows firsthand from a vision that this is true (the author and audience saw the same thing).

Argument 3

The law's end is punishment, which is the opposite of the Atonement's end, which is happiness (v. 10).

Evidence 1

There needs to be an opposition in all things. If not so, righteousness could not be brought to pass, neither wickedness, neither holiness nor misery, neither good nor bad. Wherefore, all things must needs be a compound in one; wherefore, if it should be one body it must needs remain as dead, having no life neither death, nor corruption nor incorruption, happiness nor misery, neither sense nor insensibility (v. 11).

Persuasion Strategy	Argument Type	Evidence Type
Logos	Induction	Subjective

Lehi uses a subjective inductive argument. He believes the binary option of eternal punishment or eternal happiness arises from the need for opposition in all things.

Evidence 2

Without opposition in all things, our existence has no purpose (v. 12).

Persuasion Strategy	Argument Type	Evidence Type
Logos	Abduction	Subjective

Lehi builds on the necessity of an opposition in all things to mean a purpose for being. This is a subjective abductive claim since our having a purpose does not necessarily follow from the reality of an opposition in all things, despite Lehi's belief.

Evidence 3

Without opposition in all things, God's wisdom, eternal purposes, power, mercy, and justice are destroyed (v. 12).

Persuasion Strategy	Argument Type	Evidence Type
Logos	Abduction	Subjective

Lehi provides another subjective abductive claim since he believes God's wisdom, eternal purposes, power, mercy, and justice are destroyed without opposition in all things.

Evidence 4

And if ye shall say there is no law, ye shall also say there is no sin. If ye shall say there is no sin, ye shall also say there is no righteousness. And if there be no righteousness, there be no happiness. And if there be no righteousness nor happiness, there be no punishment nor misery. And if these things are not, there is no God. And if there is no God we are not, neither the earth; for there could have been no creation of things, neither to act nor to be acted upon; wherefore, all things must have vanished away (v. 13).

Persuasion Strategy	Argument Type	Evidence Type
Logos	Induction	Subjective

This subjective inductive claim is constructed as a series of causes and correlations. It is inductive since each point does not necessarily result in the counterpoint. But it is plausible, especially in Jacob's worldview.

Evidence 5

The Lord God gave unto man that he should act for himself. Wherefore, man could not act for himself save it should be that he was enticed by the one or the other (v. 16).

Persuasion Strategy	Argument Type	Evidence Type
Logos	Induction	Subjective

Lehi's premise that God gave man free agency is an inductive argument since it cannot be proven. The second half of this evidence is very close to being objective since it is self-evident in many cases.

Argument 4

If Adam had not transgressed, he would not have fallen, but he would have remained in the garden of Eden. And all things which were created must have remained in the same state in which they were after they were created; and they must have remained forever, and had no end (v. 22).

Evidence 1

They would have had no children; wherefore they would have remained in a state of innocence, having no joy, for they knew no misery; doing no good, for they knew no sin (v. 23).

Persuasion Strategy	Argument Type	Evidence Type
Logos	Abduction	Subjective

Lehi's premise is based on an observation of humanity where we can experience joy and misery, and know good and sin. He contrasts this with Adam's state before the fall. He concludes that Adam would not have experienced these things unless he transgressed.

Evidence 2
Adam fell that men might be; and men are, that they might have joy (v. 25).

Persuasion Strategy	Argument Type	Evidence Type
Logos	Induction	Subjective

In one of the most beautiful passages in all of scripture, Lehi provides a "big picture" of why we are here on earth and of our purpose: Adam fell so that we may exist, and we exist to have "joy." If Adam had not transgressed, he would not have fallen. But because of his fall, the Messiah shall come to redeem the children of men. And it is the Messiah's actions that lead to our joy.

This is an inductive argument, but a claim can be made that it is an abductive one.

Argument 5
The Messiah redeems humanity from the fall (v. 26).

Evidence 1
And because they are redeemed from the fall, they have become free forever, knowing good from evil, to act for themselves and not to be acted upon (v. 26).

Persuasion Strategy	Argument Type	Evidence Type
Logos	Abduction	Subjective

Lehi's logic in this Subjective-Abductive argument is compelling: Humanity's ability to know good and evil is due to being "free forever" from the fall because of the Messiah's redemption.

This independence of humanity is bi-directional – it originates from Christ's infinite Atonement and goes backward in time to Adam and forward into the limitless future. It covers all humans for all time.

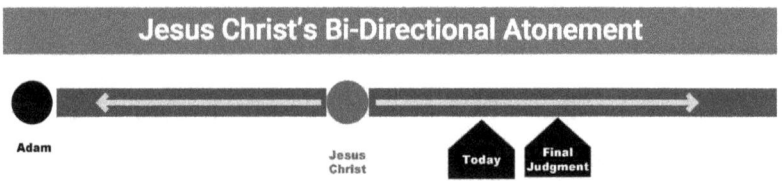

Jesus Christ's *infinite* Atonement covers all humans for all time

Figure 5: The Scope of Jesus Christ's Atonement

Evidence 2

[Humans can] act for themselves and not to be acted upon save it be by the punishment of the law at the great and last day (v. 26).

Persuasion Strategy	Argument Type	Evidence Type
Logos	Induction	Subjective

Lehi switches back to an inductive argument with the belief that humans have the innate ability to act for themselves and not be acted upon. God will never force anyone to be good, and any external constraint that causes someone to act in a particular way is taken into consideration when we are judged.

This passage contains one of the most profound passages in all scripture: *We are free to act for ourselves and not be acted upon.* This is an insight that Viktor Frankl learned while being brutalized in Nazi concentration camps for three years.[17] It is something Richard Wurmbrand learned while being imprisoned and tortured by communists for fourteen years.[18] It is the key to living a life of meaning and enduring contentment with how we view ourselves.

---

[17] See Frankl, V. E.

[18] See Wurmbrand, R.

42   Verifiable Evidence for the Book of Mormon

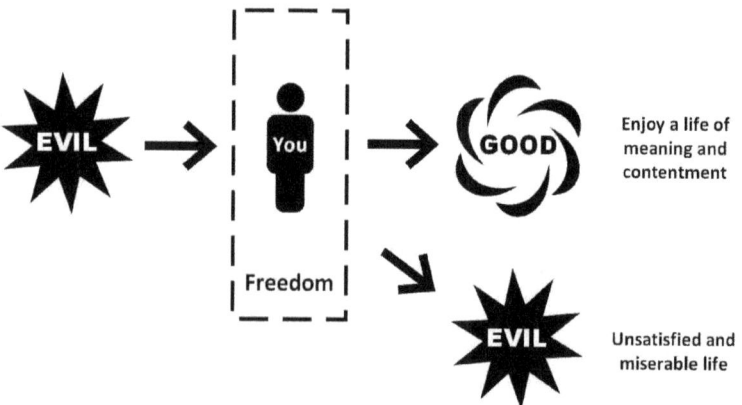

Figure 6: The Brilliance of 2 Nephi 2:26

It does not matter what others or life does to us; we have the innate freedom to choose how we respond to stimuli. And it is how we independently act and react to outside forces that determine our character.[19]

We are free to do evil just because we have received evil. For instance, we can take it out on our spouses and kids if we have a terrible day at work. Likewise, we can take advantage of others because someone took advantage of us.

But we are also free to turn the other cheek and forgive those who have harmed us. We can live lives of charity and compassion toward all, even our enemies. We are

---

[19] See Covey, S. R., and Christensen, C. M., Allworth, J., Dillon, K.

free to act unilaterally instead of passively letting others influence our happiness with ourselves.

Evidence 3

Humans are free to choose liberty and eternal life, through the great Mediator of all men, or to choose captivity and death, according to the captivity and power of the devil (v. 27).

Persuasion Strategy	Argument Type	Evidence Type
Logos	Induction	Subjective

Lehi asserts that we are free to choose liberty and eternal life through Jesus Christ or choose captivity and death. This is a Subjective-Inductive argument since it assumes we can freely choose one or the other.

Essay Conclusion

And now, my sons, I would that ye should look to the great Mediator, and hearken unto his great commandments; and be faithful unto his words, and choose eternal life, according to the will of his Holy Spirit; And not choose eternal death, according to the will of the flesh and the evil which is therein, which giveth the spirit of the devil power to captivate, to bring you down to hell, that he may reign over you in his own kingdom (v. 28-29).

Persuasion Strategy	Argument Type	Evidence Type
Ethos	Induction	Subjective

Lehi's conclusion sees a switchback to an Ethos persuasion strategy, where he gives his final wishes to his sons.

Thesis Restatement

Choose eternal life, according to the will of his Holy Spirit; And not choose eternal death, according to the will of the flesh and the evil which is therein, which giveth the spirit of the devil power to captivate, to bring you down to hell (v. 28-29).

Call to Action

Choose eternal life, according to the will of his Holy Spirit; And not choose eternal death, according to the will of the flesh and the evil which is therein, which giveth the spirit of the devil power to captivate, to bring you down to hell (v. 28-29).

Attempt to Change Worldview

1. *Adam fell that men might be; and men are, that they might have joy (v. 25).*

2. *The Messiah cometh in the fulness of time so that he may redeem the children of men from the fall. And because they are redeemed from the fall, they have become free forever, knowing good from evil, to act for themselves and not to be acted upon (v. 26).*

2 Nephi 2 Conclusion

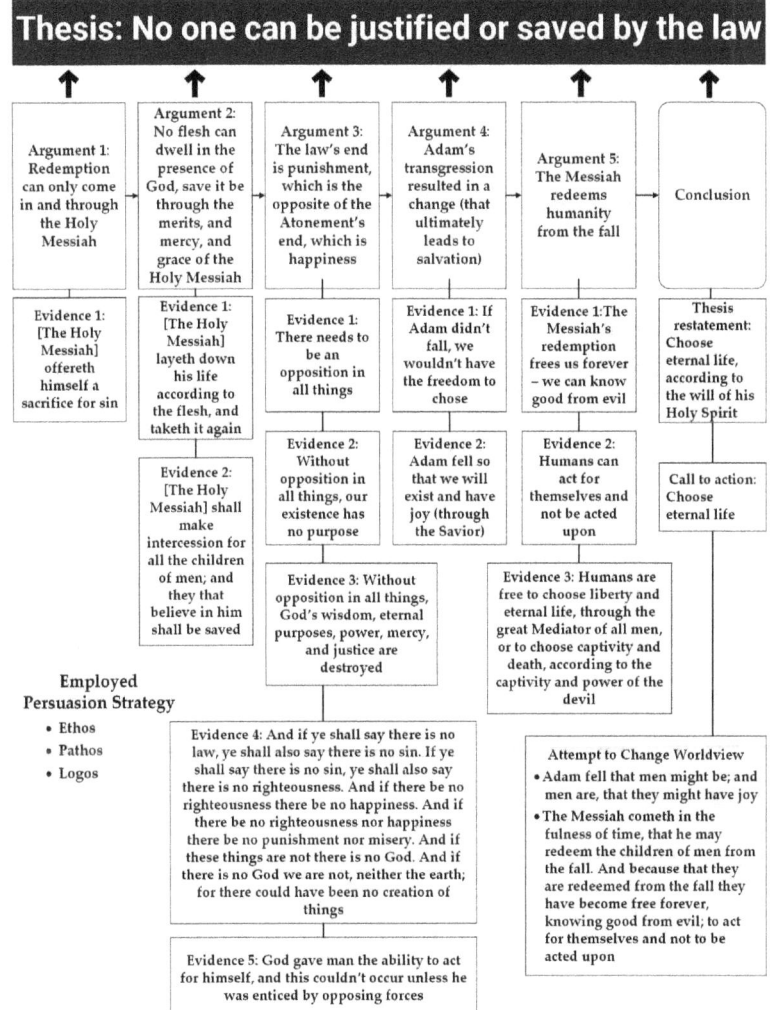

Figure 7: 2 Nephi 2's Persuasive Essay Structure

2 Nephi 2 has long been known as one of the best fonts of succinct "wisdom" expressions in the Book of Mormon. Ideas like "Adam fell that men might be; and men are, that they might have joy" and we have genuine freedom

to act for ourselves and not be acted upon are concepts that no young person like Joseph Smith is expected to come up with on their own since this level of wisdom requires a lifetime of experience. Frankl and Wurmbrand needed to be subjected to the absolute worst brutality of humanity before obtaining the same insight. Covey and Christensen needed to first know of the idea and see its applicability in the lives of thousands of peers over decades of work before using it to help others have lives of meaning.[20]

The 2 Nephi 2 essay contains a thesis statement: "No one can be justified or saved by the law" and five arguments with evidence that support the thesis. It has a conclusion that indirectly restates the thesis but directly issues a call to action and attempts to change the audience's worldview. Structurally speaking, it is clearly a persuasive essay.

Jacob's prior supernatural vision, where he saw the same thing his father and brother saw, changes the assessment of this essay's first two arguments since

---

[20] Even today, most go through their entire lives without grasping how transformative the "*[Humans are] free forever, knowing good from evil, to act for themselves and not to be acted upon*" insight is. Yet, understanding and applying it is the key to living a life of contentment. How could any 23-year-old, anywhere, come up with something so wise?

Jacob's vision becomes the evaluation criterion of that portion of his father's message. Since both the author and audience (Jacob) shared the same experience, what would typically be an inductive argument becomes deductive, and what is usually a subjective mental construct becomes objective.

Arguments 3 to 5 are intensely cerebral. They are the product of a brilliant person who spent decades contemplating the profound implications of Adam's Fall and Christ's Atonement. His exhortation was successful – his people never reverted to the traditional Jewish view that salvation only comes from ritualized observance to the Law of Moses.

2 Nephi 2's contents show clear evidence of deliberate design. The notion that an uneducated 23-year-old Joseph Smith can just dictate this chapter in a few hours is an idea that cannot be seriously entertained.

Evidence #2: Alma 32

Essay Classification: Argumentation-Missionary

Alma 32 is the beginning of Alma's protreptic effort to save a lost people. Alma was the high priest and former chief judge over the Nephites (Alma 8:11-12) who led a mission to the Zoramites around 74 BC. The Zoramites were dissenters and functioned as an autonomous group within the Nephite nation. They were apostates who rejected the belief of the coming Christ and believed they were guaranteed salvation without needing to repent. They also only prayed once a week and just in their houses of worship.

Alma's audience comprised of poor Zoramites who were prohibited from entering the synagogues to worship God. While it is never stated, it appears their concern was that they could not be saved because they could not worship God in the synagogues.

When the poor Zoramites approached him, Alma "beheld that their afflictions had truly humbled them, and that they were in a preparation to hear the word" (v. 6).

> *Therefore he did say no more to the other multitude; but he stretched forth his hand, and cried unto those whom he beheld, who were truly penitent, and said unto them: I behold that ye are lowly in heart; and if so, blessed are ye (v. 7-8).*

Alma introduced these poor Zoramites to a new worldview: They are blessed because they have become humble. He repeats it twice more so there will not be any doubt: They are blessed (v. 13-14)!

He explains why they are blessed:

> *I say unto you, it is well that ye are cast out of your synagogues, that ye may be humble, and that ye may*

learn wisdom; for it is necessary that ye should learn wisdom; for it is because that ye are cast out, that ye are despised of your brethren because of your exceeding poverty, that ye are brought to a lowliness of heart; for ye are necessarily brought to be humble.

And now, because ye are compelled to be humble blessed are ye; for a man sometimes, if he is compelled to be humble, seeketh repentance; and now surely, whosoever repenteth shall find mercy; and he that findeth mercy and endureth to the end the same shall be saved (v. 12-13).

Alma states that those compelled to become humble are blessed *if* they seek repentance and endure to the end. Alma then points out a self-evident truth: Those who humble themselves are more blessed than those forced to become humble (v. 14). He fleshes out this higher level of blessedness by including repentance and enduring to the end as requirements (v. 15-16).

Alma then makes them think of the next level by segueing into his actual essay, which starts after "in other words" in v. 16:

Blessed is he that believeth in the word of God, and is baptized without stubbornness of heart.

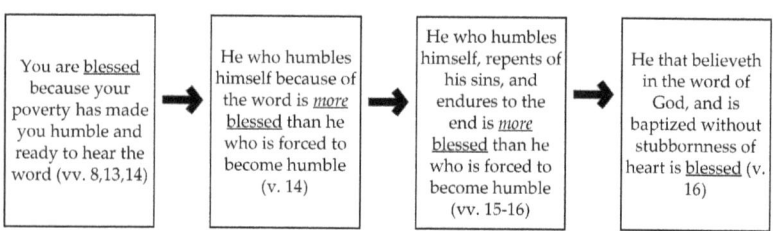

Figure 8: *Alma 32's "Blessed" Progression and Segue Into His Prepared Essay*

Thesis/Position

Blessed is he that believeth in the word of God, and is baptized without stubbornness of heart [for they shall be saved] (v. 16).

Alma's thesis statement or primary point is those who genuinely believe in the word of God shall be saved. All his arguments in this essay support this thesis.

Alma equates being blessed with being saved (v. 13), and those who believe in the word of God are those who humble themselves, repent of their sins, and endure to the end (v. 13,15).

Frame of Argument

Argument 1: Counterargument/Rebuttal

Asking for a sign to obtain surety before believing is useless (v. 17-18).

Alma starts his argument by refuting an opposing viewpoint:

Part 1: Argumentative and Persuasive Essays 51

Yea, there are many who do say: If thou wilt show unto us a sign from heaven, then we shall know of a surety; then we shall believe (v. 17).

Evidence 1

If a man knoweth a thing, he hath no cause to believe, for he knoweth it (v. 18).

Alma starts by pointing out the epistemic difference between belief and knowledge – those who know something do not need belief. This is self-evident since knowing means one has a more credible comprehension of the "Truth" based on greater perceptive awareness or much more familiarity and experience with the subject than one who only believes.

Persuasion Strategy	Argument Type	Evidence Type
Logos	Deduction	Objective

It is self-evident that knowledge is consequentially superior to belief. Our entire legal system is based on this axiom.

Evidence 2

Those who know God's will and do not do it are cursed much more than those who only have faith who then fall into sin (v. 19).

Persuasion Strategy	Argument Type	Evidence Type
Logos	Induction	Subjective

While it should be self-evident that those who "know" have greater liability for violations than those who do not know, this may or may not be the case with God. It definitely is likely, but it would not have been evident to the audience. Alma certainly believed so based on his experience and worldview.

Evidence 3

Faith is to not have a perfect knowledge of things (v. 21).

Persuasion Strategy	Argument Type	Evidence Type
Logos	Deduction	Objective

It is self-evident that those who only have "faith" in something cannot possibly have perfect knowledge of it.

Evidence 4

If ye have faith, ye hope for things that are not seen, but are true (v. 21).

Persuasion Strategy	Argument Type	Evidence Type
Logos	Induction	Subjective

To have faith is to hope for something unseen or not yet actualized. But Alma's extension into that object of faith being necessarily true is subjective since it only applies when God is the object.

After all, one can have faith in items outside God that may be true or false. A person can certainly hope that the object is actual even if the likelihood is remote (e.g., faith that one will win the lottery if he buys a ticket).

Evidence 5

Faith is not perfect knowledge—even so it is with my words. Ye cannot know of their surety at first, unto perfection, any more than faith is a perfect knowledge. But behold, if ye will awake and arouse your faculties, even to an experiment upon my words, and exercise a particle of faith, yea, even if ye can no more than desire to believe, let this desire work in you, even until ye believe in a manner that ye can give place for a portion of my words (v. 26-27).

Persuasion Strategy	Argument Type	Evidence Type
Logos	Deduction	Objective

Alma starts with a deductive argument and ends with the beginning of an argument from analogy that goes into full expression in the subsequent verses.

It is self-evident that faith is not perfect knowledge, and, in like manner, one cannot know Alma's words are true at the beginning. To know with a surety, one needs to experiment to determine whether his words are credible.

Argument 2

God wants you to believe on his word (v. 22).

Evidence 1

He imparteth his word by angels unto men, yea, not only men but women also. Now this is not all; little children do have words given unto them many times, which confound the wise and the learned (v. 23).

Persuasion Strategy	Argument Type	Evidence Type
Ethos	Induction	Objective

Alma argues that God wants us to believe in his words and claims the evidence is from angelic visitations to humans. The Zoramites would immediately know he was talking about himself and the four sons of King Mosiah (Mosiah 27:11-18). The existence of five eyewitnesses to the same event makes this objective evidence since others can confirm the angel's appearance.

Argument 3

We will compare the word unto a seed. Now, if ye give place, that a seed may be planted in your heart, behold, if it be a true seed, or a good seed, if ye do not cast it out by your unbelief, that ye will resist the Spirit of the Lord, behold, it will begin to swell within your breasts (v. 28).

Alma's third argument that those who believe in the word of God are saved is the employment of a thought experiment using the argument from analogy process (v. 28-43). His audience would have been mainly comprised of farmers, who would intimately know his analogy of the word of God being a seed. If one feels the seed grows within himself, he can conclude that it is true or good.

Evidence 1

When you feel these swelling motions, ye will begin to say within yourselves—It must needs be that this is a good seed, or that the word is good, for it beginneth to enlarge my soul; yea, it beginneth to enlighten my understanding, yea, it beginneth to be delicious to me. Now behold, would not this increase your faith? I say unto you, Yea; nevertheless, it hath not grown up to a perfect knowledge (v. 28-29).

Alma argues that when one feels the seed (the word of God) starting to "swell" within them and feels that it starts to enlarge their soul, enlighten their understanding, and taste delicious, then one's faith in the seed increases. But since this is still in the early stages – that belief has not yet grown into perfect knowledge (just like the knowledge that a freshly sprouted seed is promising, yet does not mean it is guaranteed to produce good fruit when it matures).

Persuasion Strategy	Argument Type	Evidence Type
Logos	Abduction	Subjective

This evidence's persuasion strategy is Logos and not Pathos since Alma uses the audience's mind to evaluate the effects of the changes on their emotions. It is an abduction argument where causal conclusions can be obtained from the seed's growth. The evidence type is subjective since only the person experimenting can experience the results.

Evidence 2

But behold, as the seed swelleth, and sprouteth, and beginneth to grow, then you must needs say that the seed is good; for behold it swelleth, and sprouteth, and beginneth to grow. And now, behold, will not this strengthen your faith? Yea, it will strengthen your faith: for ye will say I know that this is a good seed; for behold it sprouteth and beginneth to grow. And now, behold, are ye sure that this is a good seed? I say unto you, Yea; for every seed bringeth forth unto its own likeness (v. 30-31).

Alma moves onto the next stage where the seed has now "swelleth, and sprouteth, and beginneth to grow." He adds that when this happens, a person's knowledge is perfect "in that thing" (v. 34) – that is, only that the seed is good. The word of God has "swelled your souls ... your understanding doth begin to be enlightened, and your mind doth begin to expand" (v. 34).

Persuasion Strategy	Argument Type	Evidence Type
Logos	Abduction	Subjective

Evidence 2 is stylistically identical to Evidence 1.

Evidence 3

If a seed groweth, it is good, but if it groweth not, behold it is not good, therefore it is cast away (v. 32).

Alma pivots back to the objective fact that seeds that grow are good, and those that do not grow are bad and can be thrown away.

Persuasion Strategy	Argument Type	Evidence Type
Logos	Deduction	Objective

It is self-evident that seeds that grow are "good," and seeds that do not grow are "bad."

Evidence 4

As the tree beginneth to grow, ye will say: Let us nourish it with great care, that it may get root, that it may grow up, and bring forth fruit unto us. And now behold, if ye nourish it with much care it will get root, and grow up, and bring forth fruit (v. 37).

Persuasion Strategy	Argument Type	Evidence Type
Logos	Induction	Objective

Alma moves on to the next stage of the seed's development – where it is now a tree. He uses an induction argument where a tree is likely to bear fruit if appropriately nourished.

While the scenario is within a subjective spiritual experience, it is empirical that a tree "nourished with great care" is likely to grow up and bring forth fruit. But it is not guaranteed to do so, making this an induction argument and not a deduction.

Evidence 5

But if ye neglect the tree, and take no thought for its nourishment, behold it will not get any root; and when the heat of the sun cometh and scorcheth it, because it hath no root it withers away, and ye pluck it up and cast it out. Now, this is not because the seed was not good, neither is it because the fruit thereof would not be desirable; but it is because your ground is barren, and ye will not nourish the tree, therefore ye cannot have the fruit thereof (v. 38-39).

Persuasion Strategy	Argument Type	Evidence Type
Logos	Deduction	Objective

Alma uses another objective deductive argument that any plant that does not receive nourishment will die. And it does not matter that the tree was good – the person's neglect is responsible for the tree's death. He adds that if one's negligence was due to lacking the goal of the tree bearing fruit, then one can never eat it. Incidentally, he now mentions that the tree is the tree of life (v. 40).

Evidence 6

But if ye will nourish the word, yea, nourish the tree as it beginneth to grow, by your faith with great diligence, and with patience, looking forward to the fruit thereof, it shall take root; and behold it shall be a tree springing up unto everlasting life. And because of your diligence and your faith and your patience with the word in nourishing it, that it may take root in you, behold, by and by ye shall pluck the fruit thereof, which is most precious, which is sweet above all that is sweet, and which is white above all that is white, yea, and pure above all that is pure; and ye shall feast upon this fruit even until ye are filled, that ye hunger not, neither shall ye thirst (v. 41-42).

Persuasion Strategy	Argument Type	Evidence Type
Pathos	Induction	Subjective

Alma's final argument is a repeat and expansion of this argument's Evidence 4, which asserts that those who nourish the tree by "faith with great diligence, and with patience, looking forward to the fruit thereof" will eat its fruit that gives eternal life. He starts with an induction argument and ends with a strong pathos, where the audience can imagine eating the fruit that provides incredible happiness and eternal life. This is subjective evidence—only the person experimenting can encounter the results.

Essay Conclusion

If you nourish the word, yea, nourish the tree as it starts to grow with your faith, diligence, and patience, looking forward to its coming fruit; then the tree will take root and will become a tree springing up unto everlasting life. In just a little, you will then pluck the fruit, which is the most precious and sweetest, and whitest, and purest thing imaginable! You will feast upon the fruit until you are full and no longer hunger or thirst. Then, my brethren, you shall reap the rewards of your faith, and diligence, patience, and long-suffering, waiting for the tree to bring forth fruit unto you (v. 41-43).

Persuasion Strategy	Argument Type	Evidence Type
Pathos	Abduction	Subjective

Thesis Restatement

The word of God (the tree) will produce fruit that gives eternal life (v. 41-43).

Call to Action

Nurture the tree (the word of God) so that it will grow and produce fruit that gives eternal life (v. 37-42).

Attempt to Change Worldview

The poor Zoramites can enjoy true eternal life by exercising faith in the word (v. 41-43) instead of the false teachings of the Zoramite rulers who taught only those who prayed in their worship centers will be saved.

Alma 32 Conclusion

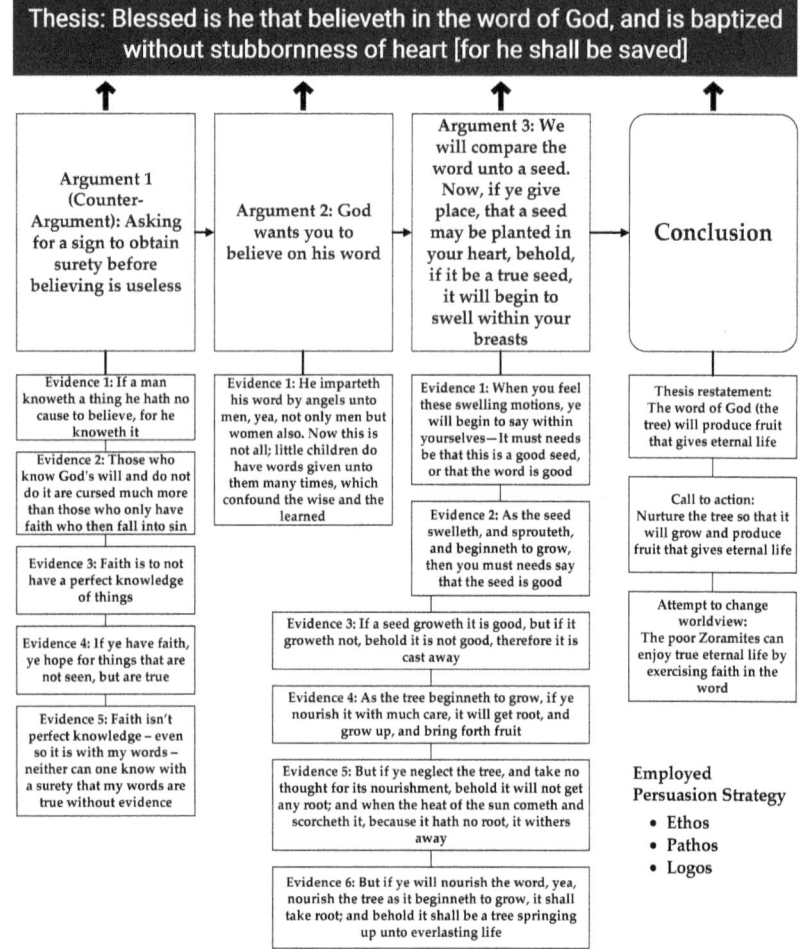

Figure 9: Alma 32's Argumentative Essay Structure

Alma 32:16-43 is a genuine argumentative essay and can be proven empirically since it contains all the components and structure of this literature type. Argument 1 was a philosophical counterargument and was refined to become coherent. Argument 2 was unsupported and could have been improved. Argument 3 shows preparation was made before preaching concerning faith and the seed as the word of God. It is tailored to an audience primarily comprised of farmers.

The essay mainly uses the Logos persuasion strategy. Ethos is only found in Argument 2 as Alma was one of those who saw God's angel, but it is implied throughout because of his status as the high priest over the Nephite nation and former chief judge. (Alma could not help but be credible to the poor Zoramites. He would not need to state his credibility – they automatically would find him credible.) Pathos is used as a finale.

It is easy to see Alma's prepared speech (v. 16-43), in which he added personalization in v. 24-25, using both Logos and Pathos. Verses 8-16 were unprepared text that specifically addressed the concerns of the newly arrived second group of Zoramites (v. 4-5). Because that portion was impromptu, it contains an argument without support or evidence (v. 14-16).

The contents and aftermath in Alma 35 show Alma addressed the target audience's needs and concerns: The poor Zoramites had a terrible self-image – they were "esteemed as filthiness/dross" by the wealthier Zoramites (v. 3) and priests who cast them out of the synagogues (v. 5) – the only place where they could worship God (v. 10). The unsaid implication is that they would be excluded from those guaranteed salvation because they were prohibited from worshiping God in their areas of worship (Alma 31:17). Alma counteracted their negative self-image by telling them repeatedly that they are actually "blessed" (v. 8,13,14) and built on this by telling them they will be even more blessed if they accept the word or the word of God (v. 14-16). He then segued into his prepared speech concerning faith and the seed as the word.

The organized structure of Alma 32:16-43 cannot be dictated by someone like Joseph Smith in just a few hours without extensive rewrites and layout changes.

Evidence #3: Alma 33

Essay Classification: Argumentation-Missionary

This chapter is the second half of Alma's preaching to the Zoramites, a people whose theology taught them that they can only worship God in their synagogues (Alma 32:5) and that there will not be any Christ or Son of God who will come (Alma 31:16-17). Alma's two arguments are rebuttals of the Zoramite theology.

Thesis Position

Zoramite theology contradicts the scriptures (v. 2).

Alma's thesis or primary point is that the theology of the Zoramites contradicts their scriptures and that they should accept what their scriptures teach. He reinforces

Part 1: Argumentative and Persuasive Essays 65

this importance in v. 12-14, where he asks them, "Do you believe those scriptures which have been written by them of old? Behold, if ye do, ye must believe what Zenos said … Now behold, my brethren, I would ask if ye have read the scriptures? If ye have, how can ye disbelieve …."

Frame of Argument

Argument 1

The Scriptures have the prophet Zenos mentioning one can pray to God anywhere (v. 3-11).

Evidence 1

The prophet Zenos prayed to God while in the wilderness, field, in his house, closet, and amid the congregations (v. 4-9).

Persuasion Strategy	Argument Type	Evidence Type
Logos	Deduction	Objective

The Zoramites can confirm that their scriptures had the prophet Zenos praying to God in multiple places, not just in their synagogues. Their worldview makes the claim deductive and objective to them.

Argument 2

The prophets in the scriptures prophesied of the Son of God (v. 11-14).

Evidence 1

The prophets Zenos and Zenock mention the Son of God (v. 11-17).

Persuasion Strategy	Argument Type	Evidence Type
Logos	Deduction	Objective

The Zoramites can confirm that their scriptures had the prophet Zenos and Zenock mentioning the Son of God.

Evidence 3

Moses used the brass serpent as a type of the Son of God (v. 19-20).

Alma argues that Moses used the brass serpent as a type of the Son of God because all who looked at the brass serpent were saved, just as all who look to the Son of God will be saved.

Persuasion Strategy	Argument Type	Evidence Type
Logos	Argument from Analogy	Subjective

While the Zoramites can confirm in their scriptures that Moses used a brass serpent to heal people (cf. Numbers 21:8-9), one must accept that Moses used the brass serpent

Part 1: Argumentative and Persuasive Essays   67

as a type of the Son of God (cf. John 3:14-15). This means this evidence is a subjective argument from analogy.

Segue 1

[The Son of God is real because] the scriptures say we receive mercy because of the Son of God (v. 11,13,16).

Alma weaves his ultimate goal into his essay: The Son of God is the reason why we receive mercy and forgiveness.

Evidence 1

The prophets Zenos and Zenock said we receive mercy because of the Son of God (v. 11,16).

Persuasion Strategy	Argument Type	Evidence Type
Logos	Deduction	Objective

The Zoramites can confirm that their scriptures had the prophet Zenos and Zenock saying we receive mercy because of the Son of God.

Evidence 2

Moses raised up a type of [the Son of God] (per Numbers 21:8-9) where people are saved just by looking at the brass serpent. Those who refused to look did so because they did not believe it would heal them (v. 19-20).

Persuasion Strategy	Argument Type	Evidence Type
Logos	Induction	Subjective

The Zoramites can confirm that their scriptures contained the story of Moses and the brass serpent, where those who looked at it were saved while those who refused perished. But because Alma claimed the brass serpent was a type of the Son of God while the source text did not explicitly say so, this makes his argument inductive and subjective.

Counterargument/Rebuttal Form

No.	Original Belief	Counterargument/ Rebuttal
1	We have no place to worship our God because we are cast out of our synagogues because of our poverty (Alma 32:5).	The prophet Zenos said in the scriptures that God listens to our prayers regardless of where we are (v. 2-12).

No.	Original Belief	Counterargument/ Rebuttal
2	There is no Christ (Alma 31:16-17).	The prophet Zenos, Zenock, and Moses in the scriptures all spoke of the Son of God [Christ] (v. 11-20).

Essay Conclusion

Cast about your eyes and begin to believe in the Son of God, that he will come to redeem his people, and that he shall suffer and die to atone for their sins; and that he shall rise again from the dead, which shall bring to pass the resurrection, that all men shall stand before him, to be judged at the last and judgment day, according to their works. And now, my brethren, I desire that ye shall plant this word in your hearts, and as it beginneth to swell even so nourish it by your faith. And behold, it will become a tree, springing up in you unto everlasting life. And then may God grant unto you that your burdens may be light, through the joy of his Son. And even all this can ye do if ye will. (v. 22-23)

Persuasion Strategy	Argument Type	Evidence Type
Pathos	Induction/Abduction	Subjective

Alma concludes his essay using Pathos – specifically, faith, joy, and anticipation within subjective evidence. He uses two argument types: Induction (for belief) and Abduction (for the causal explanation of feeling the seed swell within a person).

Thesis Restatement
Believe the scriptures (v. 12).

Read the scriptures / it is written (v. 14-19).

Call to Action
Cast your eyes upon the Son of God and be saved (v. 21-22).

Plant this word in your hearts (v. 23).

Attempt to Change Worldview
If you plant the word in your heart and nourish it by your faith, then it will become a tree, springing up in you unto everlasting life. Your burdens will become light through the joy of God's Son (v. 23).

Alma 33 Conclusion

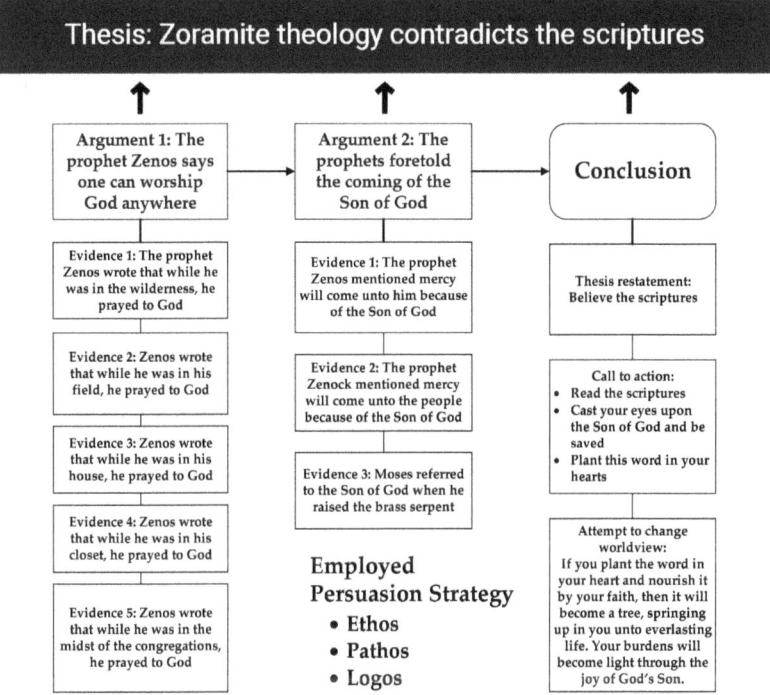

Figure 10: Alma 33's Argumentative Essay Structure

The counterargument-driven argumentative essay of Alma 33:2-23 starts with Alma ignoring the Zoramites' questions in v. 1. And the reason why Alma ignored their questions is that they could not be integrated into his hastily prepared speech.

The structure of the two counterarguments (the scriptures teach we can pray to God anywhere, and the scriptures mention the Son of God) are not as developed as Alma's preaching in Alma 32:17-43 or Amulek's preaching in Alma 34:9-16 and Alma 34:32-41. This shows Alma lacked time to refine the logic and possibly did not have additional written resources to enhance the references by the time of his speech. It appears likely that this essay was done while they were in the land of the Zoramites, and the other essays found in Alma 32 and 34 were already written and refined speeches that were brought with them on their missionary journey (which were then customized for their audience).

One can see Alma "champing at the bit" to share his primary idea: **Mercy comes because of the Son of God** (v. 11,13,16). He used the story of Moses and the brass serpent as a type of Christ, where the mere act of looking at the figure saves. He painted a vivid picture that some Israelites were *stupid* and died because they could not be bothered to do something simple – just *look* at the brass serpent. He then expands on the story by paralleling the Israelites who perished to warn those who refuse to believe in the Son of God (v. 19-22). The implication is that anyone who refuses to believe in the Son of God is just as stupid as those ancient Israelites who refused to look at the brass serpent. The lack of belief dooms both groups. The pairing and usage of negative Pathos, while crude, appears to be effective.

The most impressive part of the entire essay is his summary of the Christ-centric portion of the Gospel[21] in v. 22:

If so, wo shall come upon you; but if not so, then cast about your eyes and begin to believe in the Son of God, that he will come to redeem his people, and that he shall suffer and die to atone for their sins; and that he shall rise again from the dead, which shall bring to pass the resurrection, that all men shall stand before him, to be judged at the last and judgment day, according to their works.

This is so well developed that it appears to have gone through numerous revisions to explain how such a broad topic was summarized so succinctly and brilliantly. The Holy Bible does not have any passage describing the Gospel better using fewer words.

Table 1: Alma 33:22 – the Most Condensed Description of the Gospel in the Scriptures

Jesus Christ, According to the Gospel	
Holy Bible (Aggregate)	**Alma 33:22**
1. He is the Son of God	1. He is the Son of God

---

[21] The Gospel has two sides. The first side is on what Christ is, what he did, and what he will do. The second is on what we are required to do. See Footnote 22 for both halves.

Jesus Christ, According to the Gospel	
Holy Bible (Aggregate)	**Alma 33:22**
2. He is the Creator of the universe, Earth, and humanity	
3. He is "God" by nature	
4. He obeyed his Father's will and became human to redeem us from the Fall	4. He will come to redeem his people
5. He suffered and died for us	5. He shall suffer and die to atone for their sins
6. He rose from the dead to destroy death itself and make all humans immortal physical beings	6. He shall rise again from the dead, which shall bring to pass the resurrection
7. He will then judge all humankind at the Last Day	7. All men shall stand before him, to be judged at the last and judgment day, according to their works
8. He conjoined the divine and human natures so that his grace allows some humans to be "adopted" by God, share ultimate glory, and participate in God's very nature, mutual-indwelling, and oneness	

Alma 33:22 is a phenomenal passage – no other verse in the Bible contains so much detail about the Gospel. Five of the eight most notable Christ-centric doctrines are found in just a single verse.

While the argumentative essay of Alma 33:2-23 was not refined, its organized structure cannot be dictated by someone like Joseph Smith without rewrites and layout changes. For example, it is a near-certainty that even someone highly knowledgeable in the scriptures cannot summarize the Christ-centric portion of the Gospel the same way Alma did in v. 22 without cheating by first reading the passage.[22]

---

[22] People tend to equate their denomination's theology with the "Gospel." In contrast, the biblical Gospel or Good News can be summed up as:

God's only Son, JESUS CHRIST, the Creator of the universe who is "God" by nature – obeyed his Father's will and became human flesh. He then suffered and died to annul the Fall – when Adam and Eve transgressed and inflicted sin, death, moral weakness, and trials on humanity.

He rose from the dead to destroy death itself and make all humans immortal physical beings. He will then judge all humankind at the Last Day according to our works.

He conjoined the divine and human natures so that his grace allows some humans to be "adopted" by God, share ultimate glory, and participate in God's very nature, mutual-indwelling, and oneness.

Evidence #4: Alma 34

Essay Classification: Argumentation-Expository

Amulek in Alma 34 builds on Alma's two essays to the Zoramites (in Alma 32 and 33, respectively).

The "word" that Amulek refers to is the "Word of God." The Zoramite audience was taught that they had the word of God, but their theology did not include a "Son of God" or a "Christ" (Alma 31:16-17).

Thesis/Position

The word is in Christ, the Son of God, unto salvation (v. 5-6).

Amulek starts building an argumentative essay on this foundation, which can be reworded as:

Jesus Christ, the Son of God, is the source of salvation.

This is Amulek's thesis statement, and all his arguments are designed to support it.

Frame of Argument

Argument 1

The prophets foretold Christ's coming (v. 7).

All who come unto JESUS CHRIST, repent of their sins, get baptized in his name, strive to live his teachings whereby the Holy Spirit within them continually refines and purifies them, and endure to the end will be rewarded with eternal bliss in his kingdom.

This is a restatement of what they just heard in Alma 33, where Alma told them their own prophets foretold the coming of the Son of God.

Evidence 1

Alma provided evidence that Zenos, Zenock, and Moses taught Christ, the Son of God, would come (v. 7 cf. Alma 33:11-19).

Persuasion Strategy	Argument Type	Evidence Type
Logos	Deduction	Objective

The Zoramites can confirm in their scriptures that these prophets foretold Christ's coming. Their worldview that their scriptures are theologically and historically "true" makes this a deductive and objective piece of evidence.

Argument 2

Christ will come and atone for humanity (v. 8).

Evidence 1

The Lord God said so (v. 8).

Persuasion Strategy	Argument Type	Evidence Type
Ethos	Deduction	Subjective

Amulek argues that Christ will come and atone for humanity but does not explain how he knows God said so. This means his deductive statement lacks warranted evidence and is thus subjective without clarifying information. Amulek's persuasion strategy is an indirect Ethos since he was credible due to his association with Alma.

It appears likely that Evidence 1 is merely a dangling introduction to the expository body of his essay. If so, then it was not crucial for him to justify his evidence. But he definitely could have done better than just saying, "God said so."

Argument 3
Humanity will perish unless the Son of God performs an Atonement (v. 9).

Evidence 1
Only an infinite Atonement by the Son of God saves humanity (v. 9-16).

Persuasion Strategy	Argument Type	Evidence Type
Logos	Induction	Objective

Amulek's Argumentation-Expository essay starts in v. 8. Its expository style results in objective evidence for the audience's worldview because they held that the Brass Plates' narrative was objective historical fact. This is also because using "infinite" means Christ's Atonement covers all humans for all time. Anything "infinite," by definition, includes all. V. 9 kicks off the Logos persuasion strategy where "an infinite and eternal sacrifice" that is not an animal or human sacrifice is needed to atone for "all mankind" because "all are fallen and are lost, and must perish except" an atonement pays the price for their sins.

Evidence 2

No one can sacrifice their life to pay for the sins of another. This is why the law of the nation, which is just, will not kill the brother of a murderer (v. 11-12).

Persuasion Strategy	Argument Type	Evidence Type
Logos	Deduction/Induction	Objective

The Zoramites know their law does not take the life of the brother of a murderer because an innocent man's life cannot be taken as payment for the sins of a murderer. This is an objective fact and deductive evidence based on their enacted laws.

Amulek uses an induction argument in concluding that only an infinite atonement can pay for the sins of the world because no human life can atone for another's sins.

Evidence 3

The sacrifices of the Law of Moses will be fulfilled (v. 13-14).

Persuasion Strategy	Argument Type	Evidence Type
Logos	Induction	Subjective

Amulek continues his expository essay by stating the sacrifices from the Law of Moses will eventually end because of the Son of God's sacrifice. This is subjective – his belief – since he could not provide objective evidence.

Evidence 4

The Atonement allows Mercy to satisfy the demands of Justice (v. 15-16).

Persuasion Strategy	Argument Type	Evidence Type
Logos	Deduction	Objective

Amulek uses a deductive argument – there is no epistemic uncertainty to the resolution of the contradiction of God being a just God and a merciful God when "God" – that is, Jesus Christ, pays the price of all of humanity's sins for all time. This sacrifice satisfies the demand of Justice that all "sin" be punished and then creates a new condition for Mercy to take effect on the same sinful humans. This is objective since the "infinite" Atonement of Jesus Christ, by definition, covers all humans for all time.

Amulek crafts one of the best explanations of the relationship between justice and mercy anywhere in all of scripture (only bested by Alma in Alma 42). The Son of God's infinite and eternal Atonement pays the price for all humans for all time (v. 9-10). As a result, justice is satisfied because every sin's cost was paid in full by the Son of God's sacrifice. Mercy is given to those who believe in his name (v. 15). Only those who have "faith unto repentance" who "call upon his holy name" (v. 16-17) will receive mercy. Those who refuse to exercise "faith unto repentance are exposed to the whole law of the demands of justice." (v. 16)

Jesus Preserves God's Justice and Mercy

```
           What is                           What is the
            God,                           Christian God,
           Morally?                           Morally?
         ┌────┴────┐                      ┌──────┴──────┐
         ▼         ▼                      ▼             ▼
        Just  ≠  Merciful                Just    =    Merciful
         │         │                      └──────┬──────┘
         ▼         ▼                             ▼
      Sinners   Sinners              Jesus Christ's Infinite
      Not Saved  Saved            Substitutionary Sacrifice On
                                     Behalf of All Humans
                                   ┌──────────┴──────────┐
                              Reject Jesus and    Accept Jesus and
                               His Conditions     His Conditions
                                   ▼                     ▼
                               Sinners               Sinners
                               Not Saved              Saved
```

Figure 11: Christ's Infinite Atonement Resolves the Just and Merciful God Contradiction

This resolves the dilemma of the contradiction between God as a "just" God and a "merciful" God.

Amulek crafts a brilliant solution to a problem that has vexed humanity for thousands of years. Without Christ's *infinite* Atonement, God cannot be a just God and merciful God at the same time.

Argument 4

This life is the time for mankind to repent. If one postpones repenting, that person cannot be saved (v. 32).

Evidence 1

When we are dead, we keep the same spirit or attitude that we have in life (v. 34).

Persuasion Strategy	Argument Type	Evidence Type
Pathos-Kairos	Induction	Subjective

Amulek uses Pathos for the first time and an induction argument to explain why people must repent while still alive:

> *Ye cannot say, when ye are brought to that awful crisis, that I will repent, that I will return to my God. Nay, ye cannot say this; for that same spirit which doth possess your bodies at the time that ye go out of this life, that same spirit will have power to possess your body in that eternal world (v. 34).*

This is subjective since Amulek assumes this is the case because it seems self-evident that sins stemming from the weaknesses of the flesh cannot be repented when one is dead and no longer in possession of a physical body. For example, if we die being a slave to lust, then we still have the same lustful urges after death. If we die with hatred in our hearts, then we will still have that same hatred in the afterlife. If we lived without charity in our soul, then we would still be uncharitable after death.

Amulek's point is our innate nature does not change just because we die. It is an elegant solution to the "deathbed repentance" problem, where outward professions of faith and righteousness are unaccompanied by actions. Those who are the type of person who will show genuine humility and repentance if only given a chance will find salvation, while those who will not demonstrate them if given the opportunity shall not be saved.

Kairos is also employed where the audience is pressured to repent while they still can.

Evidence 2

If we procrastinate our repentance until death, we become subject to the devil (v. 35).

Persuasion Strategy	Argument Type	Evidence Type
Pathos-Kairos	Abduction	Objective

Amulek uses an abduction argument where he asserts that those who procrastinate their repentance until it is too late become subject to the devil. He came to this conclusion because the Lord said he does not dwell in unholy temples but only in the hearts of the righteous (v. 36). If the person does not belong to the Lord, then he must belong to the devil. This is objective based on the Nephites' worldview, since the scriptures contain many passages that mention the fate of unrepentant sinners (1 Nephi 14:3-4; 15:29; 2 Nephi 2:29; 9:16,34; 28:15,21; Alma 30:60; cf. Malachi 4:1; Matthew 13:41-42; Mark 9:43; 2 Thessalonians 1:8; Revelation 20:15; 21:8).

He employed Pathos, specifically dread, to motivate people to repent while they still could.

Evidence 3

God said he does not dwell in unholy temples (v. 36).

Persuasion Strategy	Argument Type	Evidence Type
Pathos	Deduction	Objective

This is an appeal to a recognized authority, which is the scriptures. The Zoramites should repent because their scriptures say God will not dwell in unholy temples (cf. Mosiah 2:37).

Amulek uses the justification for his Evidence 2 as his Evidence 3, with its own deductive argument.

Evidence 4
The righteous have God dwelling in them, and they will sit down in his kingdom (v. 36).

Persuasion Strategy	Argument Type	Evidence Type
Pathos	Deduction	Objective

Amulek continues his Pathos persuasion strategy and uses a deductive argument by appealing to the Zoramite scriptures. The audience can confirm in their scriptures that it teaches the idea that the righteous will have God dwelling in them and they will sit down in his kingdom (cf. 1 Nephi 10:21; 15:33-35; 2 Nephi 2:8; Mosiah 2:41; 15:23) where their garments are made white through the blood of the Lamb (cf. 1 Nephi 12:10-11).

Evidence 5
Work out your salvation with fear before God (v. 37).

Persuasion Strategy	Argument Type	Evidence Type
Pathos	Deduction	Subjective

Amulek's final evidence for his fourth argument is a Pathos call to action add-on to his essay, which ended in v. 36.

Note: Amulek's essay shows he's highly cerebral and would have been comfortable in Classical Greece.

Counterarguments/Rebuttals

Audience's position	Amulek's refutation
1. There is no Christ (Alma 31:16).	1. The prophets (that the Zoramites believed in) testified of Christ (v. 6-7,33).
2. The Zoramites do not need to repent and rely upon Christ because they are guaranteed salvation (Alma 31:17).	2. Logic tells us that Christ must come since only an infinite Atonement can save all of humanity (v. 9-16).

Audience's position	Amulek's refutation
3. They only need to pray once a week and can only worship God in the synagogues (Alma 31:12-23; 32:5,11).	3. The Zoramites can worship God anywhere (v. 17-27 cf. Alma 33:2-11).

Note: Both 1 & 2 mean the Zoramites must repent and accept Christ, or else they cannot be saved.

Counterargument forms:

1. Removal of the opponent's support
2. Exposure of the opponent's faulty logic
3. Demonstration that the opponent has no support

Essay Conclusion

Repent and accept Christ. Do not harden your heart, for now is the time and day of your salvation (v. 30-31). Do not delay because if you do, you will become subject to the devil instead of dwelling with God forever (v. 35-36). Humble yourselves and worship God wherever you are (v. 38). Pray continually and patiently bear your afflictions for if you do, you shall one day rest from all your afflictions (v. 39-41).

Persuasion Strategy	Argument Type	Evidence Type
Pathos	Deduction	Objective

This is objective within the worldview of the Zoramites since they can confirm in their scriptures that if they do not repent in this life, they cannot be saved.

Thesis Restatement

1. *Repent and do not harden your heart, for now is the time and the day of your salvation [by accepting Christ] (v. 30-31).*

2. *Work out your salvation with fear before God, and no longer deny the coming of Christ (v. 37).*

3. *Stop contending against the Holy Ghost, but receive it, and take upon you the name of Christ (v. 38).*

Call to Action

1. *Exercise your faith unto repentance and cry unto the Lord (v. 17-30).*

2. *Become charitable. Otherwise, your prayers will be in vain, and you will be cast out (v. 28-29).*

3. *Now is the time to repent – do not procrastinate until it is too late (v. 31-37). Accept the Holy Spirit and the name of Christ. Repent and pray continually. Be patient, and do not revile others (v. 38-41).*

Attempt to Modify the Audience's Worldview

1. *The Scriptures testify of Christ (v. 30).*
2. *Many witnesses testify of Christ (v. 33).*
3. *Christ's sacrificial blood will make the garments of his followers white (v. 36).*
4. *Christ will come (v. 37).*
5. *Only the infinite Atonement of Jesus Christ can cause Mercy to satisfy the demands of Justice. Those who refuse to repent are exposed to the whole punishment that Justice imposes (v. 16).*
6. *Pray continually and everywhere (v. 17-27) instead of once a week and only in the synagogues (per Alma 31:12,23; 32:5,9-11).*
7. *Have hope that you will one day rest from all your afflictions (v. 41).*

Alma 34 Conclusion

Unlike Alma's missionary essays in Alma 32-33, Amulek's essay style is expository and used within a proselyting event. Alma's compositions "hook" the audience's attention while Amulek's wields the "hammer" to close the conversion to Christ. This tag-team process was likely very successful, and it is doubtful that it would have been as effective in reverse.

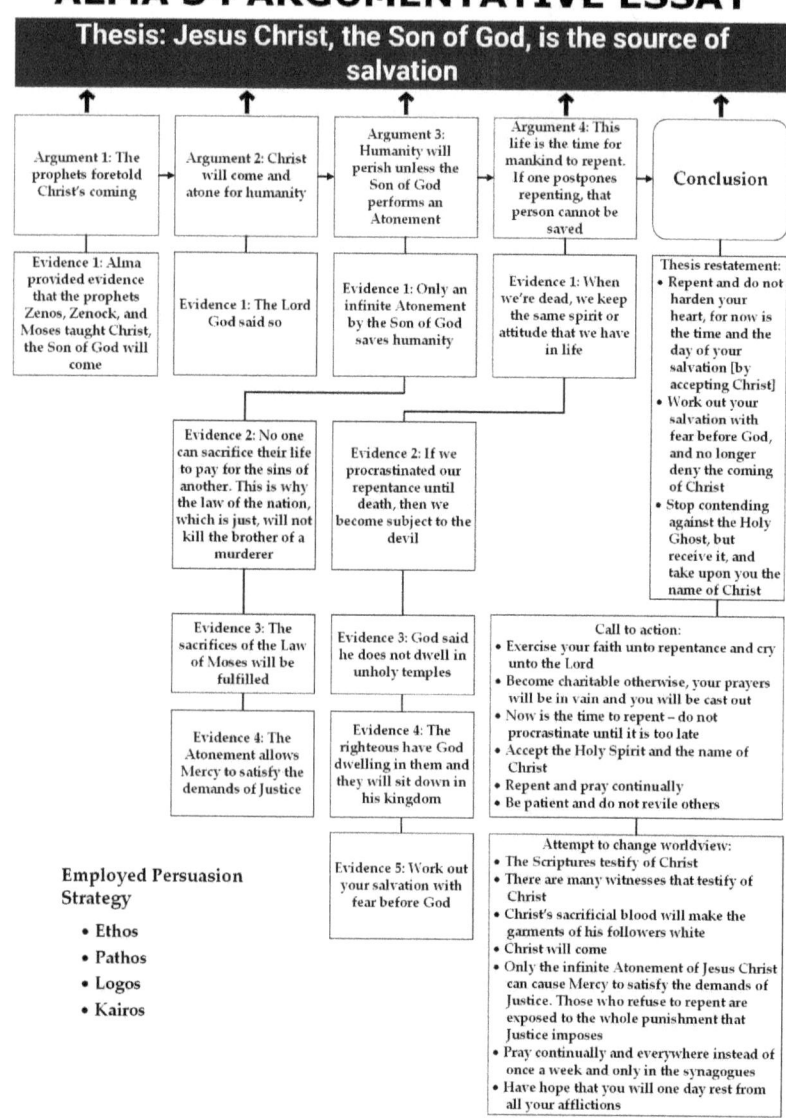

Figure 12: Alma 34's Argumentative Essay Structure

Alma 34 has a thesis statement. It has a frame of argument with four distinct argument/evidence pairs. It contains all types of persuasion strategies (Ethos, Pathos, Logos, and even Kairos). It includes three counterarguments. It has a conclusion where the thesis was restated, issued a call to action, and made the audience look at the world differently. It is clearly and unmistakably a coherent argumentative essay centered on the fact that Jesus Christ is the source of salvation.

The counterarguments show preparation was made before preaching concerning prayer and the infinite Atonement. Argument 1 was unrehearsed and appears to be an impromptu reinforcement of Alma's words in Alma 33. The contents and structure of Arguments 3 and 4 show they were written and refined before preaching.

It appears Amulek's preaching in Alma 34:9-16 and Alma 34:32-36 were combined initially, and Amulek inserted v. 17-31 after learning what the Zoramites believed and what Alma was going to say about it in Alma 33:2-11. He then edited v. 33 to harmonize the insert. He specifically used the word "dross" in v. 29 as a counterpoint to its use in Alma 32:2 (the poor are not dross because of their poverty, they will be dross if they do not remember to be charitable). Amulek then added v. 37-41 as personalization to the Zoramite audience.

The ideas found in Amulek's writings show he was one of the most profound thinkers in the Book of Mormon. Amulek quickly picked up highly complex ideas from Alma since their first contact in Alma 8:19-22. He became Alma's companion, and his first recorded preaching occurred in Alma 10-11. His exchange with Zeezrom (Alma 11:21-46) reveals a very sharp mind but lacked the skill to create a three-dimensional literary structure that Alma possessed, which is shown by the absence of an argumentative essay in that passage. After that incident, he obviously learned persuasion from Alma since Alma 34 is a masterclass example of an argumentative essay. He may have been a better writer than Alma by the quality of the "prayer" verses in v. 17-27, which were clearly written after Alma's prayer passages in Alma 33:2-11 but significantly better. Not only did he insert it in the middle of his prepared text, but he also added v. 28-31 to bridge the very different thoughts and rewrote v. 33 to make all four text blocks flow better together. It was an impressive accomplishment.

The contents of Alma 34 are so well developed and advanced that it is ludicrous to allege anyone could dictate Alma 34. The human brain does not work that way.

Part 1: Conclusion

This paper has demonstrated that argumentative and persuasive essays exist in the Book of Mormon. Anyone who has had to create them knows it is not possible to dictate them in just a few hours outside a classroom setting where the structure and methodology are fresh in mind. What lawyer, scientist, patent writer, or literary critic today can dictate argumentative essays in just a few hours or days, using all four rhetorical modes and six different content styles especially using a "dictated first draft is the final draft" process where they cannot revise the documents after dictation? And this difficulty increases exponentially when placed in the same conditions as Joseph Smith, with his education and life circumstances as a poor young farmer and laborer in 1829.

And Joseph Smith did not produce just one argumentative and persuasive essay from dictation; he dictated 46, using all four rhetorical modes and multiple content styles. So, what explains this empirical impossibility?

Appendix 1: Glossary

Argument – A series of premises that seek to demonstrate or determine the degree of truth of a conclusion. Types:

- **Deduction** – An argument where the premise or premises are true and prove the conclusion is valid with no epistemic uncertainty.

- **Induction** – A defeasible argument where the premise or premises provide some evidence that the conclusion is likely valid.

- **Abduction** – A logical inference that seeks to provide the simplest and most likely explanation that fits an observation or observations.

- **Argument from Analogy** – An argument whereby a perceived similarity or similarities between two dissimilar objects are used to support a conclusion.

- **Reductio ad absurdum** – An argument for a claim that shows its opposite would result in absurdity or error.

Argumentative Essay – A type of literature that aims to convince the audience to believe the author or align with the author's position. It uses persuasion strategies within a logical structure comprised of a thesis, a frame of argument that includes a counterargument/rebuttal, and a conclusion.

Essay – A form of writing where the author transfers organized information to the audience. An essay can be argumentative, descriptive, expository, reflective, formulaic, procedural, narrative, cause and effect, dialectic, or compare and contrast.

Objective Evidence – Evidence that can be independently confirmed.

Persuasion Strategy – A method used to convince someone. There are three types and one methodology:

- **Ethos** – A persuasion strategy that relies on the author's credibility to convince the audience.

- **Pathos** – A persuasion strategy that uses emotions or feelings to convince the audience.

- **Logos** – A persuasion strategy that uses logic to convince the audience.

- **Kairos** – A methodology that employs at least one of the three persuasion types within a sense of urgency to convince the audience (i.e., sales pressure, limited time window, the boss is coming).

Persuasive Essay – A type of literature that aims to convince the audience to believe the author or align with the author's position. It uses persuasion strategies within a logical structure comprised of a thesis, a frame of argument that does *not* include a counterargument/ rebuttal, and a conclusion.

Subjective Evidence – Evidence that cannot be independently confirmed. Its credibility is contingent upon the claimant's reputation.

Three-dimensional Literature – Literature whose persuasion requires internal logical support, such as by using a thesis statement, credible argument/evidence pairs, and a conclusion that supports the thesis statement. The most common types of three-dimensional writings today are argumentative and persuasive essays.

Two-dimensional Literature – Any form of writing that persuades or satisfies the reader without using logic. Some examples include novels, stories, poems, comics, and humor.

Part 1: Argumentative and Persuasive Essays 97

Appendix 2: The Book of Mormon's Structured Essays Table

#	STRUCTURED ESSAY	LOCATION	WORD COUNT	RHETORICAL MODE	CONTENT STYLE
1	Lehi's First Essay (Lehi's Dream)	1 Nephi 8:4-35	968	Narration	Contemporary Prophetic
2	Lehi's Second Essay	2 Nephi 1:4-32	1330	Persuasion	Authoritative
3	Lehi's Third Essay	2 Nephi 2	1456	Persuasion	Expository
4	Lehi's Fourth Essay	2 Nephi 3	1168	Persuasion	Remote Prophetic
5	Nephi's First Essay (Nephi's Panoramic Vision)	1 Nephi 11:1-14:30	5356	Narration	Contemporary Prophetic/ Remote Prophetic
6	Nephi's Second Essay	1 Nephi 19:7-21	714	Description	Contemporary Prophetic
7	Nephi's Third Essay	1 Nephi 22:2-31	1442	Exposition	Contemporary Prophetic
8	Nephi's Fourth Essay (Nephi's	2 Nephi 4:15-35	732	Description	Authoritative

#	STRUCTURED ESSAY	LOCATION	WORD COUNT	RHETORICAL MODE	CONTENT STYLE
	Soliloquy and Prayer)				
9	Nephi's Fifth Essay	2 Nephi 25:1-20	1228	Persuasion	Contemporary Prophetic
10	Nephi's Sixth Essay	2 Nephi 25:21-30	471	Persuasion	Authoritative
11	Nephi's Seventh Essay	2 Nephi 26:1-11	502	Persuasion	Contemporary Prophetic
12	Nephi's Eighth Essay	2 Nephi 26:12-33	981	Argumentation	Remote Prophetic
13	Nephi's Ninth Essay	2 Nephi 28-30	2751	Argumentation	Remote Prophetic
14	Nephi's Tenth Essay	2 Nephi 31	988	Argumentation	Expository
15	Nephi's Eleventh Essay	2 Nephi 32	427	Argumentation	Expository
16	Nephi's Twelfth Essay	2 Nephi 33	646	Exposition	Remote Prophetic
17	Jacob's First Essay	2 Nephi 6:2-18	879	Description	Contemporary Prophetic/ Remote Prophetic

Part 1: Argumentative and Persuasive Essays

#	STRUCTURED ESSAY	LOCATION	WORD COUNT	RHETORICAL MODE	CONTENT STYLE
18	Jacob's Second Essay	2 Nephi 9:1-26	1305	Argumentation	Expository
19	Jacob's Third Essay	2 Nephi 9:27-54	1083	Argumentation	Expository
20	Jacob's Fourth Essay	2 Nephi 10	966	Persuasion	Expository
21	Jacob's Fifth Essay	Jacob 2-3:11	1881	Argumentation	Authoritative
22	Jacob's Sixth Essay	Jacob 4:3-18	831	Exposition	Expository
23	Jacob's Seventh Essay	Jacob 5	3758	Narration	Remote Prophetic
24	King Benjamin's Speech Part 1	Mosiah 2:9-41	1704	Argumentation	Authoritative
25	King Benjamin's Speech Part 2	Mosiah 3	1117	Argumentation	Expository
26	King Benjamin's Speech Part 3	Mosiah 4:4-30	1390	Argumentation	Expository

100   Verifiable Evidence for the Book of Mormon

#	STRUCTURED ESSAY	LOCATION	WORD COUNT	RHETORICAL MODE	CONTENT STYLE
27	King Benjamin's Speech Part 4	Mosiah 5:6-15	482	Argumentation	Expository
28	Abinadi's Speech Part 1	Mosiah 13:11-24,27-15:10a	1361	Argumentation	Contemporary Prophetic
29	Abinadi's Speech Part 2	Mosiah 15:10b-31	740	Persuasion	Expository
30	Abinadi's Speech Part 3	Mosiah 16:1-15	560	Persuasion	Expository
31	Mosiah II's Final Address	Mosiah 29:5-32	1163	Persuasion	Authoritative
32	Alma's First Essay	Alma 5	2786	Argumentation	Missionary
33	Alma's Second Essay	Alma 7	1439	Persuasion	Missionary
34	Alma's Third Essay	Alma 9:8-30	1172	Argumentation	Missionary
35	Alma's Fourth Essay	Alma 12:12-18,22-37	1144	Argumentation	Expository

Part 1: Argumentative and Persuasive Essays

#	STRUCTURED ESSAY	LOCATION	WORD COUNT	RHETORICAL MODE	CONTENT STYLE
36	Alma's Fifth Essay	Alma 13:1-30	1329	Persuasion	Expository
37	Alma's Sixth Essay (Alma's Soliloquy)	Alma 29	708	Description	Authoritative
38	Alma's Seventh Essay	Alma 32:16-43	1216	Argumentation	Missionary
39	Alma's Eighth Essay	Alma 33:2-23	776	Argumentation	Missionary
40	Alma's Ninth Essay [to Helaman]	Alma 36	1229	Persuasion	Expository
41	Alma's Tenth Essay [to Helaman]	Alma 37	2026	Persuasion	Parental
42	Alma's Eleventh Essay [to Shiblon]	Alma 38	649	Persuasion	Parental
43	Alma's Twelfth Essay [to Corianton]	Alma 39	793	Exposition	Parental

#	STRUCTURED ESSAY	LOCATION	WORD COUNT	RHETORICAL MODE	CONTENT STYLE
44	Alma's Thirteenth Essay [to Corianton]	Alma 40	1153	Argumentation	Expository
45	Alma Fourteenth Essay [to Corianton]	Alma 41	701	Argumentation	Expository
46	Alma's Fifteenth Essay [to Corianton]	Alma 42	1228	Argumentation	Expository
47	Amulek's First Essay	Alma 10:2-11	532	Narration	Authoritative
48	Amulek's Second Essay	Alma 34	1545	Argumentation	Expository
49	Captain Moroni's Threatening Letter	Alma 60	1746	Argumentation	Contemporary Prophetic
50	Nephi's First Essay (son of Helaman)	Helaman 7:13-29; 8:11-28	1396	Argumentation	Contemporary Prophetic
51	Nephi's Second Essay (son of Helaman)	Helaman 12	872	Exposition	Expository

Part 1: Argumentative and Persuasive Essays

#	STRUCTURED ESSAY	LOCATION	WORD COUNT	RHETORICAL MODE	CONTENT STYLE
52	Samuel the Lamanite's Speech Part 1	Helaman 13:5-39	1672	Argumentation	Contemporary Prophetic
53	Samuel the Lamanite's Speech Part 2	Helaman 14:2-31	1220	Persuasion	Contemporary Prophetic
54	Samuel the Lamanite's Speech Part 3	Helaman 15	825	Persuasion	Contemporary Prophetic
55	Jesus Christ's First Essay	3 Nephi 9:2-22, 10:4-7	1112	Description	Authoritative
56	Jesus Christ's Second Essay	3 Nephi 11:22-41	643	Exposition	Authoritative
57	Jesus Christ's Third Essay	3 Nephi 12-14	2700	Exposition	Authoritative
58	Jesus Christ's Fourth Essay	3 Nephi 15:3-10, 12-16:20	1513	Exposition	Authoritative
59	Jesus Christ's Fifth Essay	3 Nephi 18:5-7, 10-	851	Exposition	Authoritative

#	STRUCTURED ESSAY	LOCATION	WORD COUNT	RHETORICAL MODE	CONTENT STYLE
		16,18-25,27-35			
60	Jesus Christ's Sixth Essay	3 Nephi 20:10-23:5	3099	Exposition	Authoritative
61	Jesus Christ's Seventh Essay	3 Nephi 27:4-33	1142	Exposition	Authoritative
62	Jesus Christ's Eighth Essay	Ether 4:6-19	664	Exposition	Authoritative
63	Mormon's First Essay	3 Nephi 29-30	524	Exposition	Remote Prophetic
64	Mormon's Second Essay	Mormon 3:17-22	256	Description	Remote Prophetic
65	Mormon's Third Essay	Mormon 5:8-24	746	Description	Remote Prophetic
66	Mormon's Fourth Essay	Mormon 7	453	Exposition	Remote Prophetic
67	Mormon's Fifth Essay	Moroni 7	1881	Argumentation	Expository
68	Mormon's Sixth Essay [to Moroni]	Moroni 8	887	Argumentation	Expository

Part 1: Argumentative and Persuasive Essays

#	STRUCTURED ESSAY	LOCATION	WORD COUNT	RHETORICAL MODE	CONTENT STYLE
69	Moroni's First Essay	Mormon 8:13-41	1255	Exposition	Remote Prophetic
70	Moroni's Second Essay	Mormon 9	1561	Argumentation	Remote Prophetic
71	Moroni's Third Essay	Ether 5	226	Exposition	Remote Prophetic
72	Moroni's Fourth Essay	Ether 8:19-26	454	Description	Remote Prophetic
73	Moroni's Fifth Essay	Ether 12:6-41	1352	Argumentation	Remote Prophetic
74	Moroni's Sixth Essay	Moroni 2-6	818	Description	Authoritative
75	Moroni's Seventh Essay	Moroni 10	1149	Argumentation	Remote Prophetic
Structured Essay Word Count			91,823		
1830 BoM Word Count			269,318	29	No. of AEs
Structured Essay Percentage of the Book of Mormon			34.09%	17	No. of PEs
Argumentative/Persuasive Essay Word Count			57,136	46	Total No. of Three-Dimensional Essays
Argumentative and Persuasive Essay Percentage of the BoM:			21.22%		

Appendix 3: Proposed Empirical Study

> Note: This proposed study is only one piece of an evidence-based practice that needs to be done to quantify the Book of Mormon's creation process. The study is designed to be used as a cohort/case-controlled study and a randomized controlled trial. It is deliberately not completed as of this book's printing to allow interested parties to conduct it without prejudicing the results.
>
> Critically-appraised synopsis/synthesis and completion of at least one systematic review will still be required after the trials are completed.
>
> Those interested in conducting the study or trial are asked to send an email to ed@edwardkwatson.com to get copies of the test materials. Put "Dictation trial" in the subject line. We are seeking at least ten independent trials with no less than a hundred participants in each to conduct a meta-analysis.

This paper proposes conducting a study that examines the likelihood that average college students can produce argumentative essays by dictation, without any preparation and usage of written resources. The students are invited to participate in a trial where they verbally argue for or against a point on a subject they are passionate about, and their words are then recorded and transcribed.

The transcriptions that contain all the parts of an argumentative essay—a thesis statement, argument/evidence pairs, counterargument, and conclusion—will be identified as argumentative essays using a Go/No-Go gate assessment tool. Those who pass through the gate then undergo a secondary assessment to evaluate the essay's effectiveness using a rubric assessment apparatus.

The two assessment tools allow for the quantification of the essays to enable using statistical analysis to evaluate performance.

The study aims to quantify the dictation process Joseph Smith used in 1829 to produce the Book of Mormon. While a lot of research has occurred on the book's *contents* in the nearly two centuries since it was created, the translation process itself has been ignored as no one was able to produce an objective criterion that allows one to assess the credibility of Joseph Smith's accomplishment.

That has now been resolved. This study provides the missing piece: Argumentative essays.

As shown in Appendix 2, there are 29 argumentative essays in the Book of Mormon. They range in size from 427 words (2 Nephi 32) to 2786 words (Alma 5), with an average of 1339 words/argumentative essay. There are also 17 persuasive essays, ranging in size from 471 words (2 Nephi 25:21-30) to 2026 words (Alma 37). They have an average of 1077 words per persuasive essay.

The study will focus on the more numerous and larger word count argumentative essays since the inclusion of a counterargument makes them more complex documents. The study will use the 1545-word Alma 34 as the benchmark.

Background

"Between 7 April and early July 1829, Smith dictated the bulk of the current Book of Mormon text to Cowdery."[23]

The vast majority of the 269,318-word Book of Mormon was dictated between April 7 to July 1, 1829, or over 85 days. Most of the effort occurred on Smith's farm in Harmony, Pennsylvania (April 7 – Late May),[24] and the remainder happened on the Whitmer farm in Fayette, New York (June 1 – July 1). Excluding time off for the relocation, breaks, the effort to secure the copyright (obtained on June 11, 1829), get financing, and find a

---

[23] Skousen, R and Jensen, R. p. xxiii. Cf. xxv "The Book of Mormon manuscript was completed around the first of July 1829."

[24] Black, S. and Skinner, A. p. 89. (Faulring, S. article: *Oliver Cowdery, Book of Mormon Scribe*)

printer, the translation process took anywhere from 54-65 days,[25] or at an average pace of 4100-5000 words per day.[26]

Translation Process

Joseph Smith looked at his seer stone (usually while it was in a hat to cut off outside light) and read aloud the words

---

[25] By way of comparison, Welch, J. (2018) estimates the translation took 57 to 63 days (p. 34).

[26] Note: This estimate is different than what other scholars provide, which is a rate of 3500-4000 words per day (cf. Skousen, R. 2009, p. xii) or over a period of 67-76 days. My fewer-day estimate is due to my experience in high-volume writing and in conducting the ancillary work associated with getting work published. The scribe's mental exhaustion from high-volume transcription by hand requires a logarithmic increase in breaks and duration. There will be times when no work will get done to allow the team, especially the scribe, to recover; otherwise, productivity crashes. Evening breaks are not enough in this instance—humans need wider recharge periods. (My practice is to produce a great amount of work within a short time frame and then have days off in between to recharge from being so deep "in the zone.") The addition of other scribes at the Whitmer farm shows Cowdery was getting burned out and needing help. We can see also instances, such as in Alma 45, when Joseph Smith had to write down 28 words (Skousen, R. p. 6) because Cowdery's brain stopped functioning. I know that feeling all too well.

Also see Welch, J. (2018) for his firsthand experience with his wife and others trying to duplicate Joseph Smith's translation process (p. 38-40).

he saw in 20-30-word batches.[27] His scribe wrote the words down and then read the text block back to Smith. After Smith confirmed that the text was correct, a new batch of words appeared on the stone, and the process continued.[28]

Whenever the translation process resumed the following day or after breaks, Smith continued where he left off without asking the last line to be read back to him.[29]

After the scribe wrote down the text, the structure was fixed and was never rearranged or re-written. All edits were kept to the grammar, spelling, and mechanics realms, not content edits. In nearly all instances, copy edits only occurred within the 20-30-word text blocks while they were transcribed.

In other words, Joseph Smith's production of the Book of Mormon was structurally a "first draft is the final draft" process.

We know this because we still have 28% of the Original Manuscript and can compare the modern edition of the Book of Mormon to the version that came from Smith's mouth. The benchmark of this study, Alma 34,

---

[27] E.g., Skousen, R. (1997); Black, S. and Skinner, A. p. 90.

[28] Ibid. p. 90.

[29] Ibid. p. 90.

happens to be in the part of the original portion that still survives.[30]

Consequently, using the coherent argumentative essay of Alma 34 as a benchmark is a valid means to evaluate whether it is possible to produce viable argumentative essays following Smith's process.

A3.1 Methodology

1. Purpose

The study aims to determine whether a person can create coherent argumentative essays, such as what exists in Alma 34, following Joseph Smith's dictation process.

This is accomplished by having participants replicate Joseph Smith's actions and then assessing their output using tools that contain quantifiable conditions.

2. Hypothesis

The null hypothesis is that there is nothing unique about the Book of Mormon's translation process. The assumption is made that people can dictate coherent argumentative essays since a natural cause is logically the default for any scientific experiment.

The alternative hypothesis is that there is a statistical difference between what Joseph Smith accomplished

---

[30] Skousen, R. p. 311-316.

with the Alma 34 benchmark and what study participants can do when replicating Smith's process. If this is validated, then it becomes possible to put some statistical numbers on the likelihood of a non-natural event.

To make the study as stringent as possible, it uses a confidence interval of 99% ($\alpha = 0.01$). The study's position is that there is just a 1% probability that the null hypothesis will be rejected.

If the P-value is less than the significance level's 0.01, then we can reject the null hypothesis and accept the alternative hypothesis.

3. Hypothesis Testing and Data Collection

As the precise conditions to replicate Joseph Smith's 1829 circumstances no longer exist anywhere in the United States — we will not find 23-year-old farmers with a third-grade education living far from urban centers without access to electricity, the internet, or libraries — this study proposed using college students as test subjects instead of the more relevant unskilled laborers and farmers without high school education.

Although college students have an unfair advantage over Joseph Smith due to their access to technology, knowledge, and familiarity with literary structures, their enthusiasm to argue for their beliefs provides us with a large supply of participants.

The testing should follow Steve Crowder's *"Change My Mind"* approach,[31] where a table with a banner is displayed in a public space on campus with a controversial topic and a "change my mind" statement beneath that invites students to argue.

The topic of dispute[32] is irrelevant – the study is only interested in how the student frames their position.

Types of Responses

The study proposes two types of responses: A baseline, where the student argues naturally, without constraints. When done, the student is asked to repeat their position, but this time, to intentionally follow restrictions by using the argumentative essay structure:

- Thesis statement
- Argument/evidence pairing
- Counterargument
- Conclusion

All the components must be dictated following Joseph Smith's translation process.

---

[31] https://www.louderwithcrowder.com/search/?q=change+my+mind

[32] The only condition is that the topic should be something the student knows well and cares enough to argue about it.

Joseph Smith's Translation Process Summary

To provide an essay comparable to the 1545-word Alma 34 benchmark, the study participant must follow the same translation process conditions that Joseph Smith employed:

- 1300 to 1500 words

- No more than two hours to create

- No written or study aids. All data must be in the person's head. A stone placed in a hat can be used if they want to focus on it.

- Dictate 20-30 words at a time. After the recorder reads the text back for confirmation, the candidate resumes with another 20-30-word block.

- After the text block is confirmed, its structure cannot be changed. Furthermore, the meaning of its paragraphs and sentences cannot be altered either (no content edits or copy edits).

- No prompts or questions. The participant needs to come up with all essay components on their own.

Data Collection

Data will be captured in two ways. Each speaker will be recorded on video, and their words will be captured using speech recognition software like Nuance's Dragon Professional Individual. The Dragon text will be compared to the video to make sure each word is correctly captured.

If words are not transcribed correctly, and the video recording cannot clarify what was said, the student will be asked to explain what they said, and the correct word will be entered manually into the transcription.

Each participant will have at least one sample, the baseline. Those who agree to provide a more detailed response will have two samples. These transcription filenames will be labeled with an "A" and "B" suffix, respectively.

4. Data Analysis

Quantifiable Tool #1: Documentation Analysis Tool

After the dictations are recorded, they will be examined to see whether they are argumentative essays. To accomplish this, a documentation analysis tool called the *Argumentative/Persuasive Writing Analysis* Form will be employed. This tool allows an objective assessment of the writing and provides a quantifiable evaluation of each deliverable for statistical analysis purposes.

Argumentative/Persuasive Writing Analysis Form

Title	Click or tap here to enter text.	Wordcount	
Subject	Click or tap here to enter text.	Reference	Click or tap here to enter text.
Author Name	Click or tap here to enter text.	Audience	Click or tap here to enter text.
Perspective	Click or tap here to enter text.		
Background	Click or tap here to enter text.		
Purpose/Goal	Click or tap here to enter text.		
Form	☐ Rebuttal	☐ One-Sided	

1. Thesis Claim/Position

Click or tap here to enter text.

2. Frame of Argument

Argument 1	Click or tap here to enter text.								
Evidence	Click or tap here to enter text.								
Persuasion Strategy	☐ Ethos	☐ Pathos	☐ Logos	☐ Kairos	☐ Blend				
Argument Type	☐ Deduction	☐ Induction	☐ Abduction	☐ Argument from analogy	☐ Reductio ad absurdum				
Confirmability	☐ Objective	☐ Subjective	☐ Abstract	☐ Not possible	☐ Other				
Argument 2	Click or tap here to enter text.								
Evidence	Click or tap here to enter text.								
Persuasion Strategy	☐ Ethos	☐ Pathos	☐ Logos	☐ Kairos	☐ Blend				
Argument Type	☐ Deduction	☐ Induction	☐ Abduction	☐ Argument from analogy	☐ Reductio ad absurdum				
Confirmability	☐ Objective	☐ Subjective	☐ Abstract	☐ Not possible	☐ Other				

Part 1: Argumentative and Persuasive Essays 117

Argument 3	Click or tap here to enter text.							
Evidence	Click or tap here to enter text.							
Persuasion Strategy	☐ Ethos		☐ Pathos		☐ Logos		☐ Kairos	☐ Blend _____
Argument Type	☐ Deduction		☐ Induction		☐ Abduction		☐ Argument from analogy	☐ Reductio ad absurdum
Confirmability	☐ Objective		☐ Subjective		☐ Abstract		☐ Not possible	☐ Other
Argument 4	Click or tap here to enter text.							
Evidence	Click or tap here to enter text.							
Persuasion Strategy	☐ Ethos		☐ Pathos		☐ Logos		☐ Kairos	☐ Blend _____
Argument Type	☐ Deduction		☐ Induction		☐ Abduction		☐ Argument from analogy	☐ Reductio ad absurdum
Confirmability	☐ Objective		☐ Subjective		☐ Abstract		☐ Not possible	☐ Other
If rebuttal, opposition's position	Click or tap here to enter text.							
Was concession made of opposition's valid points?						☐ Yes		☐ No
Counterarguments	Click or tap here to enter text.							
Form of counter-arguments	☐ Removal of the opponent's support			☐ Exposure of the opponent's faulty logic			☐ Show the opponent has no support	

3. Conclusion

Click or tap here to enter text.

Was the thesis restated?	☐ Yes	☐ No
Click or tap here to enter text.		
Was there a call to action?	☐ Yes	☐ No
Click or tap here to enter text.		
Did it intend to make the audience think or look at the world or themselves in a different way?	☐ Yes	☐ No
Click or tap here to enter text.		

4. Performance Assessment — Score (Yes = 1)

a) In your opinion, was the author credible *to the target audience*, given their worldview?					☐ Yes		☐ No	
Why?	Click or tap here to enter text.							
b) Did the author address *the target audience's* needs or concerns?					☐ Yes		☐ No	
Why?	Click or tap here to enter text.							
c) Was the author credible *to you*, given your worldview?					☐ Yes		☐ No	
Why?	Click or tap here to enter text.							
d) What was the main persuasion strategy?	☐	Ethos (Author's credibility)	☐	Pathos (Audience's emotions)	☐	Logos (Audience's mind)	☐	Kairos (Sales pressure)

5. Is it a Genuine Argumentative or Persuasive Essay? — Score (Yes = 1)

a) Does the text contain a single Thesis Claim/Position?	☐ Yes	☐ No	
b) Does it have arguments supported by evidence?	☐ Yes	☐ No	
c) Does the text contain counterarguments?	☐ Yes	☐ No	
d) Does the conclusion restate the thesis?	☐ Yes	☐ No	
e) Is there a call to action?	☐ Yes	☐ No	
f) Does it give the recipient a different perspective?	☐ Yes	☐ No	
TOTAL SCORE (Max: 8 points)			

CONCLUSION

Click or tap here to enter text.

Name	Click or tap here to enter text.	Date	Click or tap here to enter a date.
Class	Click or tap here to enter text.	Teacher	Click or tap here to enter text.

The tool functions as a Go/No-Go gate. Only the transcriptions that are objectively argumentative essays (Section 5's a, b, and c and at least one of the d, e, and f questions are answered with a "Yes") proceed to the next evaluation stage.

The transcriptions that are shown to be legitimate argumentative essays can now be evaluated on their effectiveness. This gives each essay a second quantifiable score that can be subject to statistical analysis individually and in comparison to Joseph Smith's performance.

Quantifiable Tool #2: Argumentative Essay Assessment Rubric

The second quantifiable tool is a rubric that examines the effectiveness of the argumentative essay.[33] It follows the logic found within reputable universities (e.g., Yale) to grade submissions.[34]

---

[33] This study's rubric is specific for an argumentative essay that contains a counterargument. For persuasive essays without a counterargument, ignore the refutation criteria component.

[34] This study's rubric is adapted from Yale University's *Rubric for the Assessment of the Argumentative Essay* (https://pier.macmillan.yale.edu/sites/default/files/files/Argumentative%20essay%20rubric.pdf).

Author Name: _____   **Document:** _____

Argumentative Essay Assessment Rubric

Category	3	2	1	0	Score
1. Introduction Background/history, the definition of the problem, and the Thesis Statement (the main idea, argument, or position that the author wants the audience to accept/believe)	The introductory paragraph(s) provides a detailed background or history, a clear explanation or definition of the problem, and a clear thesis statement.	The introductory paragraph(s) contains some background information and states the problem but does not provide details. It states the essay's thesis.	The introduction states the thesis but does not adequately explain the problem's background. The problem is stated but lacks detail.	The thesis or problem is vague or unclear. Background details are a seemingly random collection of information or unclear/unrelated to the topic.	

Argumentative Essay Assessment Rubric

Category	3	2	1	0	Score
2. Frame of Argument — Argument-Evidence pairing	Two or more main arguments are well developed, with each having one or more pieces of evidence. Refutation paragraph(s) acknowledges the opposing view, summarizes their main points and refutes the opposing view.	Two or more main arguments are present but may lack detail and viable evidence. Refutation paragraph(s) acknowledges the opposing view but doesn't summarize their points or refute the opposing view.	Two or more main arguments, but all lack evidence or development. Refutation paragraph(s) missing or vague.	Less than two main arguments, with poor development of ideas. Refutation is missing or vague.	

Argumentative Essay Assessment Rubric

Category	3	2	1	0	Score
3. Conclusion Restatement of the thesis, a call to action, or makes the audience think or look at the world or themselves differently	The conclusion does at least two of the following: 1. Summarizes or restates the thesis or the main topics. 2. Issues a call to action. 3. Makes the audience consider a different worldview. The author's ideas	The conclusion does one of the following: 1. Summarizes or restates the thesis or the main topics. 2. Issues a call to action. 3. Makes the audience consider a different worldview. The author's ideas are incompletely	The conclusion summarizes the main topics but is repetitive or lacks structure. No suggestions for change or opinions are included.	The conclusion does not adequately summarize the main points. No suggestions for change or opinions are included.	

Part 1: Argumentative and Persuasive Essays

Argumentative Essay Assessment Rubric

Category	3	2	1	0	Score
	are logical and well thought out.	developed.			
4. Organization Layout and progression of ideas	The essay contains a logical and compelling progression of ideas that enhance and showcase the thesis and moves the reader through the text. The structure of thought flows so smoothly that the reader hardly thinks about it.	The essay's organization is logical for the most part. The ideas are credible and transition effectively despite being rough. The ideas are not necessarily complementary, and neither are they stacked on one another to reinforce	The progression of ideas in the essay is awkward yet moves the reader through the text without too much confusion. The author sometimes lunges ahead too quickly or spends too much time on details that do not matter. Transitions appear	The essay's arrangement is unclear and illogical. The writing lacks a clear sense of direction. Ideas, details, and events seem strung together loosely or randomly. There is no identifiable internal structure, and readers have	

Argumentative Essay Assessment Rubric

Category	3	2	1	0	Score
	Complementary ideas are stacked on one another to enhance the support of the thesis. Effective, mature, and graceful transitions exist throughout the essay.	the thesis.	sporadically but not equally throughout the essay.	trouble following the author's line of thought. There are a few forced transitions in the essay, or no transitions are present.	
5. Persuasion Effectiveness Effective use of logos, ethos,	When applicable, the essay avoids logical fallacies when utilizing logos. It uses ethos, pathos, and	The essay contains at least one logical fallacy but correctly uses ethos, pathos,	The essay contains several logical fallacies. Its ethos subject lacked credibility; its	The essay is not persuasive at all.	

Argumentative Essay Assessment Rubric

Category	3	2	1	0	Score
pathos, and kairos	kairos correctly	and kairos.	pathos is awkward and transparent; or its kairos is poorly executed.		
6. Sources and Source Material	Sources and source material are clearly identified and smoothly integrated into the text.	Sources and source material are used but are not explicitly identified to the audience.	Sources and source material are used but poorly integrated into the essay. Some sources lack credibility.	The essay lacks sources and source material.	
7. Thought Articulation and Flow	The essay's thought components are	The essay's thought components are	The essay's thought components are	The essay's thought components are	

Argumentative Essay Assessment Rubric

Category	3	2	1	0	Score
Thought component development and thought module growth	phrased, expanded, reinforced, and segmented in an understandable and logical manner. Thought modules effectively conjoin to make a larger point.	phrased, expanded, reinforced, and segmented moderately well but can be significantly improved upon editing. Thought modules can conjoin to make a larger point but do so awkwardly and require additional support that is	phrased, expanded, reinforced, and segmented poorly and without a good enough reason. It is difficult to conjoin thought modules to make a larger point.	not articulated properly. Most are incomplete or isolated. The thought modules cannot be joined to make a larger point due to lacking an adhesive interface.	

Part 1: Argumentative and Persuasive Essays   127

Argumentative Essay Assessment Rubric

Category	3	2	1	0	Score
8. Typeset Logic Theme grouping and content	The essay's overall structure is logical. Section and subsection themes are coherent and contain the correct content.	The essay's overall structure is coherent, but some sections or subsections are out of the logical sequence. Some subsections contain content that is irrelevant to the subsection's theme.	The essay's overall structure is barely discernable. Sections and subsections are visible, but many of their contents are irrelevant to the section and subsection's themes.	The essay's overall structure has no discernable logic. Ideas are not grouped within sections and subsections. Paragraph blocks contain a lot of irrelevant information.	lacking.

Argumentative Essay Assessment Rubric

Category	3	2	1	0	Score
9. Body Appearance Paragraph structure, sentence syntax	The essay's paragraph blocks share the same themes and grouped ideas. Its sentences are laid out correctly.	The essay's themes do not reside in connecting paragraph blocks (another theme interrupts the primary theme's flow). Sentence syntax is generally correct. Some structurally awkward sentences exist.	Work contains some structural weaknesses and confusing syntax.	Work contains multiple incorrect paragraph structures and sentence syntax errors.	

Part 1: Argumentative and Persuasive Essays   129

Argumentative Essay Assessment Rubric

Category	3	2	1	0	Score
10. Grammar and Mechanics Grammar, punctuation, spelling, and capitalization	The essay's grammar, punctuation, spelling, and capitalization are correct.	The essay has one or two grammatical, punctuation, spelling, and capitalization errors.	The essay has three or four grammatical, punctuation, spelling, and capitalization errors.	The essay has five or more grammatical, punctuation, spelling, and capitalization errors.	

TOTAL SCORE (Max: 30)

GRADE EQUIVALENT

A	A-	B+	B	B-	C+	C	C-	D	F
28-30	26-27	25	24	23	22	21	20	18-19	17 or less

Note: While "10. Grammar and Mechanics" are important for an argumentative essay's credibility, the criterion is irrelevant to the Book of Mormon since its translation process forestalls the need to use it for comparative purposes. Consequently, any essay evaluation for comparative purposes to the Book of Mormon does not need it, and the criterion can be ignored. This means the maximum score for the second tool is 27, not 30.

All argumentative essays will contain two scores (e.g., 8:25). The first determines whether the transcription is an actual argumentative essay—and they are the only ones that go through the second tool.

Transcriptions that fail the first quantifiable tool are excluded from going through the rubric assessment since they are not argumentative essays. Their score would have a zero ("0") as the second number (e.g., 3:0).

All assessed transcriptions and argumentative essays have their scores placed on a scatterplot for linear regression and compared to the Alma 34 benchmark's 8:25 score (see A3.2 Study Benchmark: Alma 34 below). This allows for the quantification of the results using statistical analysis.

5. Conclusion

The study will conclude with the results of the data analytics.

6. Communication of Results

The study's results will be published in an academic journal, within a book, or in a subsequent revision of this book.

A3.2 Study Benchmark: Alma 34

This study uses the 1545-word Alma 34 as a benchmark to compare the participants' essays. This allows for an "apples-to-apples" comparison for the generation of quantifiable statistical analysis.

Quantifiable Tool #1 Results

The documentation analysis tool allows for creating an objective Yes/No quantifiable value to Alma 34. The tool shows the following:

Argumentative/Persuasive Writing Analysis Form

Title	Amulek's Speech to the Zoramites	Wordcount	1545
Subject	Jesus Christ saves humanity	Reference	Alma 34
Author Name	Joseph Smith (Amulek)	Audience	Zoramites (Nephite apostates)
Perspective	Amulek believes he is charged to preach the Gospel to the Zoramites to bring them back to the true faith.		
Background	The land of Zoram was a province in the Nephite nation that separated after the dissolution of the monarchy. The separation also had the Zoramites leaving the true faith and establishing their own religion. Alma (the Nephite religion's high priest and former chief judge) and his assistant, Amulek, went to preach to the Zoramites in the hopes of enticing them back to Christ.		
Purpose/Goal	Convince the Zoramites to return to the True Church		
Form	☒ Rebuttal	☐ One-Sided	

1. Thesis Claim/Position

The word is in Christ, the Son of God, unto salvation (v. 5-6).

2. Frame of Argument

Argument 1	The prophets foretold Christ's coming (v. 7).							
Evidence	Alma provided evidence that Zenos, Zenock, and Moses taught Christ that the Son of God would come (v. 7 cf. Alma 33:11-19).							
Persuasion Strategy	☐ Ethos	☐ Pathos	☒ Logos	☐ Kairos	☐ Blend			
Argument Type	☒ Deduction	☐ Induction	☐ Abduction	☐ Argument from analogy	☐ Reductio ad absurdum			
Confirmability	☒ Objective	☐ Subjective	☐ Abstract	☐ Not possible	☐ Other			
Argument 2	Christ will come and atone for humanity (v. 8).							
Evidence	The Lord God said so (v. 8).							
Persuasion Strategy	☒ Ethos	☐ Pathos	☐ Logos	☐ Kairos	☐ Blend			

Part 1: Argumentative and Persuasive Essays   133

Argument Type	☒ Deduction	☐ Induction	☐ Abduction	☐ Argument from analogy	☐ Reductio ad absurdum
Confirmability	☐ Objective	☒ Subjective	☐ Abstract	☐ Not possible	☐ Other

Argument 3	Humanity will perish unless the Son of God performs an Atonement (v. 9).
Evidence 1	Only an infinite Atonement by the Son of God saves humanity (v. 9-16).

Persuasion Strategy	☐ Ethos	☐ Pathos	☒ Logos	☐ Kairos	☐ Blend ———
Argument Type	☐ Deduction	☒ Induction	☐ Abduction	☐ Argument from analogy	☐ Reductio ad absurdum
Confirmability	☒ Objective	☐ Subjective	☐ Abstract	☐ Not possible	☐ Other

Evidence 2	No one can sacrifice their life to pay for the sins of another. This is why the law of the nation, which is just, will not kill the brother of a murderer (v. 11-12).

Persuasion Strategy	☐ Ethos	☐ Pathos	☒ Logos	☐ Kairos	☐ Blend ———
Argument Type	☒ Deduction	☒ Induction	☐ Abduction	☐ Argument from analogy	☐ Reductio ad absurdum
Confirmability	☒ Objective	☐ Subjective	☐ Abstract	☐ Not possible	☐ Other

Evidence 3	The sacrifices of the Law of Moses will be fulfilled (v. 13-14).

Persuasion Strategy	☐ Ethos	☐ Pathos	☒ Logos	☐ Kairos	☐ Blend ———
Argument Type	☐ Deduction	☒ Induction	☐ Abduction	☐ Argument from analogy	☐ Reductio ad absurdum
Confirmability	☐ Objective	☒ Subjective	☐ Abstract	☐ Not possible	☐ Other

Evidence 4	The Atonement allows Mercy to satisfy the demands of Justice (v. 15-16).

Persuasion Strategy	☐ Ethos	☐ Pathos	☒ Logos	☐ Kairos	☐ Blend ———
Argument Type	☒ Deduction	☐ Induction	☐ Abduction	☐ Argument from analogy	☐ Reductio ad absurdum
Confirmability	☒ Objective	☐ Subjective	☐ Abstract	☐ Not possible	☐ Other

Argument 4	This life is the time for mankind to repent. If one postpones repenting, that person cannot be saved (v. 32).

Verifiable Evidence for the Book of Mormon

Evidence 1	When we're dead, we keep the same spirit or attitude that we have in life (v. 34).								
Persuasion Strategy	☐ Ethos		☐ Pathos		☐ Logos		☐ Kairos		☒ Blend — Pathos-Kairos
Argument Type	☐ Deduction		☒ Induction		☐ Abduction		☐ Argument from analogy		☐ Reductio ad absurdum
Confirmability	☐ Objective		☒ Subjective		☐ Abstract		☐ Not possible		☐ Other

Evidence 2	If we procrastinate our repentance until death, we become subject to the devil (v. 35).								
Persuasion Strategy	☐ Ethos		☐ Pathos		☐ Logos		☐ Kairos		☒ Blend — Pathos-Kairos
Argument Type	☐ Deduction		☐ Induction		☒ Abduction		☐ Argument from analogy		☐ Reductio ad absurdum
Confirmability	☒ Objective		☐ Subjective		☐ Abstract		☐ Not possible		☐ Other

Evidence 3	God said he does not dwell in unholy temples (v. 36).								
Persuasion Strategy	☐ Ethos		☒ Pathos		☐ Logos		☐ Kairos		☐ Blend —
Argument Type	☒ Deduction		☐ Induction		☐ Abduction		☐ Argument from analogy		☐ Reductio ad absurdum
Confirmability	☒ Objective		☐ Subjective		☐ Abstract		☐ Not possible		☐ Other

Evidence 4	The righteous have God dwelling in them, and they will sit down in his kingdom (v. 36).								
Persuasion Strategy	☐ Ethos		☒ Pathos		☐ Logos		☐ Kairos		☐ Blend —
Argument Type	☒ Deduction		☐ Induction		☐ Abduction		☐ Argument from analogy		☐ Reductio ad absurdum
Confirmability	☒ Objective		☐ Subjective		☐ Abstract		☐ Not possible		☐ Other

Evidence 5	Work out your salvation with fear before God (v. 37).								
Persuasion Strategy	☐ Ethos		☒ Pathos		☐ Logos		☐ Kairos		☐ Blend —

Part 1: Argumentative and Persuasive Essays 135

Argument Type	☒ Deduction	☐ Induction	☐ Abduction	☐ Argument from analogy	☐ Reductio ad absurdum
Confirmability	☐ Objective	☒ Subjective	☐ Abstract	☐ Not possible	☐ Other

If rebuttal, opposition's position 1	There is no Christ (Alma 31:16).		
Was concession made of the opposition's valid points?		☐ Yes	☒ No
Counterargument 1	The prophets (that the Zoramites believed in) testified of Christ (v. 6-7,33).		
Form of counterargument	☒ Removal of the opponent's support	☒ Exposure of the opponent's faulty logic	☒ Show the opponent has no support
Opposition's position 2	The Zoramites do not need to repent because they are guaranteed salvation (Alma 31:17).		
Was concession made of the opposition's valid points?		☐ Yes	☒ No
Counterargument 2	Logic tells us that Christ must come since only an infinite Atonement can save all of humanity (v. 9-16).		
Form of counterargument	☐ Removal of the opponent's support	☒ Exposure of the opponent's faulty logic	☐ Show the opponent has no support
Opposition's position 3	They only need to pray once a week and can only worship God in the synagogues (Alma 31:12-23; 32:5,11).		
Was concession made of the opposition's valid points?		☐ Yes	☒ No
Counterargument 3	The Zoramites can worship God anywhere (v. 17-27 cf. Alma 33:2-11).		
Form of counterargument	☒ Removal of the opponent's support	☒ Exposure of the opponent's faulty logic	☒ Show the opponent has no support

3. Conclusion

Repent and accept Christ. Do not harden your heart, for now is the time and day of your salvation (v. 30-31). Do not delay because if you do, you will become subject to the devil instead of dwelling with God forever (v. 35-36). Humble yourselves and worship God wherever you are (v. 38). Pray continually and patiently bear your afflictions for if you do, you shall one day rest from all your afflictions (v. 39-41).		
Was the thesis restated?	☒ Yes	☐ No

1. Repent and do not harden your heart, for now is the time and the day of your salvation [by accepting Christ] (v. 30-31).
2. Work out your salvation with fear before God, and no longer deny the coming of Christ (v. 37).
3. Stop contending against the Holy Ghost, but receive it, and take upon you the name of Christ (v. 38).

Was there a call to action?	☒ Yes	☐ No

1. Exercise your faith unto repentance and cry unto the Lord (v. 17-30).
2. Become charitable. Otherwise, your prayers will be in vain, and you will be cast out (v. 28-29).
3. Now is the time to repent – do not procrastinate until it is too late (v. 31-37). Accept the Holy Spirit and the name of Christ. Repent and pray continually. Be patient, and do not revile others (v. 38-41).

Did it intend to make the audience think or look at the world or themselves in a different way?	☒ Yes	☐ No

1. The Scriptures testify of Christ (v. 30).
2. Many witnesses testify of Christ (v. 33).
3. Christ's sacrificial blood will make the garments of his followers white (v. 36).
4. Christ will come (v. 37).
5. Only the infinite Atonement of Jesus Christ can cause Mercy to satisfy the demands of Justice. Those who refuse to repent are exposed to the whole punishment that Justice imposes (v. 16).
6. Pray continually and everywhere (v. 17-27) instead of once a week and only in the synagogues (per Alma 31:12,23; 32:5,9-11).
7. Have hope that you will one day rest from all your afflictions (v. 41).

4. Performance Assessment			Score (Yes = 1)
a) In your opinion, was the author credible *to the target audience*, given their worldview?	☒ Yes	☐ No	1
Why?	The poor Zoramites recognized Alma's prominence in their society. He was the first chief judge and high priest over the entire nation after the monarchy was abolished (comparable to being the president and pope at the same time). As the only remaining witness to the appearance of the angel that upended their nation, Alma would be the most famous person they knew. Amulek, by virtue of being Alma's companion, would automatically be considered credible by the audience.		

Part 1: Argumentative and Persuasive Essays

b) Did the author address *the target audience's* needs or concerns?		☒ Yes ☐ No		1
Why?	The poor Zoramites had a very poor self-image from being cast out of their synagogues and being unable to worship God. As their religion taught that only those belonging to the Zoramite religion can be saved, and they can only pray to God within their synagogues, the implication is that the poor Zoramites were afraid that they cannot be saved. Amulek and Alma addressed their fears; they are not "dross" but are blessed. They can worship God anywhere, and only Christ can save them.			
c) Was the author credible *to you*, given your worldview?		☒ Yes ☐ No		
Why?	I agree with Amulek's thesis and arguments			
d) What was the main persuasion strategy?	Ethos ☐ (Author's credibility)	Pathos ☐ (Audience's emotions)	Logos ☒ (Audience's mind)	Kairos ☐ (Sales pressure)

5. Is it a Genuine Argumentative or Persuasive Essay?		Score (Yes = 1)
a) Does the text contain a single Thesis Claim/Position?	☒ Yes ☐ No	1
b) Does it have arguments supported by evidence?	☒ Yes ☐ No	1
c) Does the text contain counterarguments?	☒ Yes ☐ No	1
d) Does the conclusion restate the thesis?	☒ Yes ☐ No	1
e) Is there a call to action?	☒ Yes ☐ No	1
f) Does it give the recipient a different perspective?	☒ Yes ☐ No	1
TOTAL SCORE (Max: 8 points)		8

CONCLUSION	
The 1545-word Alma 36 is a genuine argumentative essay.	

Name	Click or tap here to enter text.	Date	Click or tap to enter a date.
Class	Click or tap here to enter text.	Teacher	Click or tap here to enter text.

The Documentation Analysis Tool gives Alma 34 a score of 8 points, out of a maximum of 8. There is no doubt that it is a coherent argumentative essay.

Quantifiable Tool #2 Results

The rubric allows for the creation of a second quantifiable value to Alma 34. But unlike the other tool's Yes/No gated process, the rubric provides a more nuanced assessment of the essay's effectiveness.

The rubric shows the following concerning Alma 34:

Author Name	Joseph Smith (Amulek)	Document	The Book of Mormon, Alma 34

Argumentative Essay Assessment Rubric

Category	3	2	1	0	Score
1. Introduction Background/ history, the definition of the problem, and the Thesis Statement (the main idea, argument, or position that the author wants the audience to accept or believe)	The introductory paragraph(s) provides a detailed background or history, a clear explanation or definition of the problem, and a clear thesis statement.	The introductory paragraph(s) contains some background information and states the problem but does not provide details. It states the essay's thesis.	The introduction states the thesis but does not adequately explain the problem's background. The problem is stated but lacks detail.	The thesis or problem is vague or unclear. Background details are a seemingly random collection of information or unclear/unrelated to the topic.	3
2. Frame of Argument Argument-Evidence pairing	Two or more main arguments are well developed, with each having one or more pieces of evidence. Refutation paragraph(s) acknowledges the opposing view, summarizes their main points and refutes the opposing view.	Two or more main arguments are present but may lack detail and viable evidence. Refutation paragraph(s) acknowledges the opposing view but doesn't summarize their points or refute the opposing view.	Two or more main arguments, but all lack evidence or development. Refutation paragraph(s) missing or vague.	Less than two main arguments, with poor development of ideas. Refutation is missing or vague.	3

Argumentative Essay Assessment Rubric

Category	3	2	1	0	Score
3. Conclusion Restatement of the thesis, a call to action, or makes the audience think or look at the world or themselves differently	The conclusion does at least two of the following: 1. Summarizes or restates the thesis or the main topics. 2. Issues a call to action. 3. Makes the audience consider a different worldview. The author's ideas are logical and well thought out.	The conclusion does one of the following: 1. Summarizes or restates the thesis or the main topics. 2. Issues a call to action. 3. Makes the audience consider a different worldview. The author's ideas are incompletely developed.	The conclusion summarizes the main topics but is repetitive or lacks structure. No suggestions for change or opinions are included.	The conclusion does not adequately summarize the main points. No suggestions for change or opinions are included.	3
4. Organization Layout and progression of ideas	The essay contains a logical and compelling progression of ideas that enhance and showcase the thesis and moves the reader through the text. The structure of thought flows so smoothly that the reader hardly thinks about it.	The essay's organization is logical for the most part. The ideas are credible and transition effectively despite being rough. The ideas are not necessarily complementary, and neither are they stacked on one another to reinforce the	The progression of ideas in the essay is awkward yet moves the reader through the text without too much confusion. The author sometimes lunges ahead too quickly or spends too much time on	The essay's arrangement is unclear and illogical. The writing lacks a clear sense of direction. Ideas, details, and events seem strung together loosely or randomly. There is no identifiable internal structure, and	2

Argumentative Essay Assessment Rubric

Category	3	2	1	0	Score
	Complementary ideas are stacked on one another to enhance the support of the thesis. Effective, mature, and graceful transitions exist throughout the essay.	thesis.	details that do not matter. Transitions appear sporadically but not equally throughout the essay.	readers have trouble following the author's line of thought. There are a few forced transitions in the essay, or no transitions are present.	
5. Persuasion Effectiveness Effective use of logos, ethos, pathos, and kairos	When applicable, the essay avoids logical fallacies when utilizing logos. It uses ethos, pathos, and kairos correctly	The essay contains at least one logical fallacy but correctly uses ethos, pathos, and kairos.	The essay contains several logical fallacies. Its ethos subject lacked credibility; its pathos is awkward and transparent; or its kairos is poorly executed.	The essay is not persuasive at all.	2
6. Sources and Source Material	Sources and source material are clearly identified and smoothly integrated into the text.	Sources and source material are used but are not explicitly identified to the audience.	Sources and source material are used but poorly integrated into the essay. Some sources lack credibility.	The essay lacks sources and source material.	3
7. Thought Articulation	The essay's thought	The essay's thought	The essay's thought	The essay's thought	3

Argumentative Essay Assessment Rubric

Category	3	2	1	0	Score
and Flow Thought component development and thought module growth	components are phrased, expanded, reinforced, and segmented in an understandable and logical manner. Thought modules effectively conjoin to make a larger point.	components are phrased, expanded, reinforced, and segmented moderately well but can be significantly improved upon editing. Thought modules can conjoin to make a larger point but do so awkwardly and require additional support that is lacking.	components are phrased, expanded, reinforced, and segmented poorly and without a good enough reason. It is difficult to conjoin thought modules to make a larger point.	components are not articulated properly. Most are incomplete or isolated. The thought modules cannot be joined to make a larger point due to lacking an adhesive interface.	
8. Typeset Logic Theme grouping and content	The essay's overall structure is logical. Section and subsection themes are coherent and contain the correct content.	The essay's overall structure is coherent, but some sections or subsections are out of the logical sequence. Some subsections contain content that is irrelevant to the subsection's theme.	The essay's overall structure is barely discernable. Sections and subsections are visible, but many of their contents are irrelevant to the section and subsection's themes.	The essay's overall structure has no discernable logic. Ideas are not grouped within sections and subsections. Paragraph blocks contain a lot of irrelevant information.	3

Argumentative Essay Assessment Rubric					
Category	3	2	1	0	Score
9. Body Appearance Paragraph structure, sentence syntax	The essay's paragraph blocks share the same themes and grouped ideas. Its sentences are laid out correctly.	The essay's themes do not reside in connecting paragraph blocks (another theme interrupts the primary theme's flow). Sentence syntax is generally correct. Some structurally awkward sentences exist.	Work contains some structural weaknesses and confusing syntax.	Work contains multiple incorrect paragraph structures and sentence syntax errors.	3
~~10. Grammar and Mechanics Grammar, punctuation, spelling, and capitalization~~	~~The essay's grammar, punctuation, spelling, and capitalization are correct.~~	~~The essay has one or two grammatical, punctuation, spelling, and capitalization errors.~~	~~The essay has three or four grammatical, punctuation, spelling, and capitalization errors.~~	~~The essay has five or more grammatical, punctuation, spelling, and capitalization errors.~~	~~0~~
			TOTAL SCORE (Max: ~~30~~ 27)		25

Note: "10. Grammar and Mechanics" is an unnecessary evaluation criterion for the Book of Mormon and any comparison with it since its dictation creation process ignores grammar and mechanics.

The rubric gives Alma 34 a score of 25 points out of a maximum of 27.

Alma 34 Score

For linear regression statistical comparison purposes, Alma 34 has an **8:25** score. This is the value of the benchmark in the scatterplot to illustrate how Joseph Smith's Alma 34 compares to today's college students' dictated argumentative essays.

Appendix 4: Argumentative and Persuasive Essay Tools

(All accessed: February 12, 2022.)

- Essay Structure (Elizabeth Abrams, ©2000, The Writing Center at Harvard University) [https://writingcenter.fas.harvard.edu/pages/essay-structure]

- Rubric for the Assessment of the Argumentative Essay (Yale University) [https://pier.macmillan.yale.edu/sites/default/files/files/Argumentative%20essay%20rubric.pdf]

- An Introduction to the Writing of Essays (Princeton University Press) [http://assets.press.princeton.edu/chapters/s7936.pdf]

- Guidelines for Writing Effective Essays (Massachusetts Institute of Technology) [https://ocw.mit.edu/courses/urban-studies-and-planning/11-225-argumentation-and-communication-fall-2006/lecture-notes/writing_eff_esay.pdf]

- Academic Writing Skills Guide (2013, Steve New [with accumulated contributions from colleagues] SAID Business School, University of Oxford) [https://weblearn.ox.ac.uk/access/content/group/159bc1ca-0c7b-454c-8aad-c6c711affc04/Documents/acadwrit2013.pdf]

- Argumentative Essays (Purdue Online Writing Lab) [https://owl.purdue.edu/owl/general_writing/academic_writing/essay_writing/argumentative_essays.html]

PART 2: ALMA 36'S MULTIFACETED STRUCTURE

Abstract

The Book of Mormon's Alma 36 is famous for its complex chiasmus as an example of why the Book of Mormon is probably authentic since the paired concept elements within a writing style likely unknown to Joseph Smith are obvious. But the precise chiastic model is uncertain since it is possible to produce anywhere from an eight-element model to a seventeen-element model, depending on the modeler's preferences and on how many word or phrase concepts are excluded to make the model appear viable.

However, the presence of chiasmus is not the only reason why this chapter is so remarkable. Alma 36 displays a layout of not one but three complete structures, each of which requires a lengthy creation process that contradicts the way it was written down, where Joseph Smith dictated to his scribe while looking at his seer stone.

This paper examines these three facets of Alma 36 that demonstrate deliberate design in a manner that cannot be done by dictation in a few hours.

First, this paper argues that Alma 36 is a persuasive essay – a type of literature that requires a three-dimensional logical structure to be coherent.

Second, this paper points out that Alma 36 is structurally a persuasive public speech that appears to be modified for Helaman as a sacred keepsake. If so, then the personalization

> *process was quick and only required changing one word six times and adding nine words to one sentence.*
>
> *Finally, this paper contends that Alma 36 is a seven-element <u>thematic chiasm</u> instead of a chiasmus based on word or phrase elements. Each theme contains one to three paired concept elements that do not need to be within a chiastic structure themselves, only within the chiastic theme.*

Introduction

The Church of Jesus Christ of Latter-day Saints ("the Church") believes the Book of Mormon is Scripture and equal to the Holy Bible. As an object that objectively exists – anyone can hold a copy in their hands and read it – the book functions as the "Gordian Knot Cutter" of Christianity by quickly narrowing down the possible candidates for the "True Church" out of the tens of thousands of Christian denominations that currently exist.[1] In simplistic terms, if the Book of Mormon is true, then The Church of Jesus Christ of Latter-day Saints is

---

[1] Barrett, et. al. identified over 33,000 Christian denominations. Each denomination claims they are the True Church or are part of it and justify its independence from the others using biblical interpretation and authority claims. The problem lies in how they can show their interpretation is correct while the interpretations of tens of thousands of other Christian denominations are wrong.

likely the True Church based on the number of people who believe the book is true.

Without the Book of Mormon, one will need to evaluate the beliefs and practices of tens of thousands of denominations to determine which one to join since each one justifies its existence with biblical interpretation and authority claims. But no other objective standard exists that allows a denomination to justify why their interpretation and authority claims are credible compared to other denominations. The Holy Bible cannot be used as an evaluation criterion since they all hold it to be their scripture. Given that people can have different opinions about the same object (e.g., "Is President Trump 'good' or 'bad'?"), one perspective cannot be validated without one or more external fixed references.

With the Book of Mormon, the search for the True Church becomes very easy instead of very hard. One merely needs to find out whether the Book of Mormon is true. If a conclusion of credibility is obtained, then one can be confident to have found the True Church. But if it is demonstrably not true, then one still has the problem of determining which denomination to join.

While receiving a personal answered prayer from God is always preferred (since nothing beats an actual communication from God), it is possible to objectively assess the Book of Mormon's credibility to a high probability. And though Hebraisms, linguistics, chiasmus, archaeology, and other empirical realms are all valid fields in which to assess the Book of Mormon's authenticity, this paper focuses on an area that does not require the readers to have specialized knowledge – only the ability to process ideas rationally, within an organized structure.

Alma 36 is the ideal exhibit to use to determine the Book of Mormon's objective credibility since, at a little over 1200 words, it is small enough that anyone can take the time to read it and study its structure, layout, and contents. Moreover, it is one of the surviving portions of the Original Manuscript[2] – the version that came directly from Joseph Smith's lips that his scribe wrote down. We can see that the structure of the current edition of Alma 36 is identical to what was dictated in 1829.

This paper examines three facets of Alma 36 that show objective evidence that it was deliberately designed:

1. It is a persuasive essay.
2. It appears to be a modified persuasive public speech.
3. It is a thematic chiasm with paired concept elements.

---

[2] Skousen, R. p. 319-325.

Part 2: Alma 36's Multifaceted Structure   151

Any of these items means it is not possible for Joseph Smith to dictate this chapter to his scribe in a few hours around April 24, 1829,[3] while he was looking at his seer stone. This creation problem becomes exponentially truer when examining all three facets as a whole.[4]

Deliberate Design or Dictated?

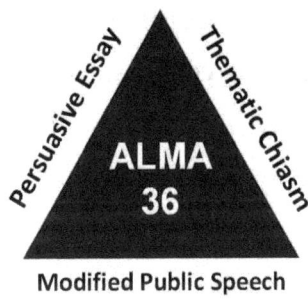

Modified Public Speech

Figure 13: Alma 36's Challenge to the World

---

[3] Welch, J. (2018). p. 42.

[4] This paper is primarily concerned with deliberate design as an objective standard instead of chiasmus since chiasmus is only an outcome of deliberate design. The empirical confirmation of deliberate design must explain how a product of deliberate design was dictated in just a few hours by Joseph Smith to Oliver Cowdery. Either Alma 36 was a product of a dictation process – which is what twelve eyewitnesses saw, and what the Church has been attacked on for nearly two centuries with Joseph Smith looking at his seer stone, or it was a product of deliberate design that was merely copied over.

Alma 36 can be duplicated. There is nothing impossible about its contents that prevents anyone from trying to create a 1229-word persuasive essay that is also a thematic chiasm with paired concept elements.

But creating one requires an organized approach, where the persuasive essay components are developed and mapped to ensure the essay is coherent. When the logic is finished, the theme blocks are outlined in chiasmus, paired words and phrases are associated with the themes, the entire document is resequenced, and text is added or deleted to complete the new layout while ensuring the essay remains coherent despite the modifications. Finally, the text is polished as a persuasive public speech.

None of this is easy, and only those familiar with specific structural writing procedures would even succeed. But even they will need to know beforehand what they are expected to write and have a detailed process to follow to create the multifaceted essay.

If Alma 36 is conclusively shown to be a deliberately designed product, then verifiable evidence exists that Joseph Smith did the impossible: he dictated a coherent, persuasive modified public speech essay in a thematic chiastic form.

What this objective impossibility means is left to the reader. But it is a sobering reminder that one cannot dismiss the Book of Mormon without thought. It exists whether we like it or not.

Facet 1: Alma 36 as a Persuasive Essay

The first facet this paper examines is whether Alma 36 is a persuasive essay – a type of literature that aims to convince the audience to believe the author or align with the author's position. This type of essay uses persuasion strategies within a logical structure comprising a thesis, a frame of argument that does not include a counterargument/rebuttal, and a conclusion.

A persuasive essay has three parts:

1. **Thesis Statement** – The main idea, argument, or position that the author wants the audience to accept or believe.

2. **The Frame of Argument** – The body of the essay comprising of at least one argument and one piece of evidence that supports the thesis.

3. **Conclusion** – The close of the essay containing a restatement of the thesis, a call to action, or makes the audience think or look at the world or themselves differently.

The frame of argument always includes at least one persuasion strategy, while the conclusion may or may not contain one.

Despite a tendency to interchange "argumentative" and "persuasive," there is a distinction between the two: the argumentative essay includes a counterargument/rebuttal while the persuasive essay does not.

The argumentative essay is a more effective convincing tool than the persuasive essay since the inclusion of a counterargument/rebuttal shows the audience that potential objections were already considered and rejected.

See Figure 2: Argumentative Essay Structure and Figure 3: Persuasive Essay Structure above for the logic of these three-dimensional literature.

Alma 36 Background

According to the Book of Mormon, Alma 36 was written at the twilight of Alma's life, anywhere from 18-26 years after his conversion to Christ stemming from an angel's supernatural appearance to him and the sons of King Mosiah. The chapter itself is Alma's conversion story, which he gave to his son, Helaman, who accompanied him on his recent mission to the Zoramites. Alma's motivation for doing so is a desire for his son to keep God's commandments and maintain strong faith and loyalty to Jesus Christ.

When conventional literary criticisms are applied to the text (specifically, New Historicism, Critical, Marxist,

Part 2: Alma 36's Multifaceted Structure 155

and Psychoanalytical theories) we can "read between the lines" and build up a picture of what the Alma 36 world looked like as well as the likely motivations and practices of Alma and the Nephite public. This allows for the conclusion that the angel's appearance was one of the most impactful events in the five-hundred-year history of the Nephite nation because it resulted in the dissolution of the monarchy and weakened the authority of the central government to such an extent that the Amlicites tried to re-establish a monarchy (Alma 2-3) and the provinces of Ammonihah (Alma 8, 14-16) and Zoram (Alma 31, 35, 43) attempted to break away.

Per Maslow's hierarchy of needs, the governance model change alone directly affected the public's physiological and safety needs since the effort to maintain the authority of a single unified nation resulted in tens of thousands of deaths. Chaos, terror, suffering, violence, and starvation were very real dangers to a large portion of the public. Even the Nephite sense of belonging would have been affected by the elimination of the monarchy — what were they as a people if they did not have a king to rule over them and tell them what to do?[5]

---

[5] The Nephite sense of identity stayed strong even when they had to escape into the wilderness and rebuild again (2 Nephi 5:5-18; Omni 1:12-19) since the presence of their ruler or king anchored their

The transition to the office of the chief judges also substantially increased individual freedom and responsibility. Since these changes were unprecedented, confusion would have been ubiquitous.

Alma 36 Within a Persuasive Essay Structure

Alma was the most prolific user of the argumentation rhetorical mode in the Book of Mormon, with 13 of the 15 structured essays he wrote falling into this category.[6] His 13 is significantly higher than Nephi (7), Jacob (4), King Benjamin (4), Lehi (3), Abinadi (3), Samuel the Lamanite (3), Moroni (3), Mormon (2), and Amulek (1). Alma's familiarity with this literary style explains why Alma 36 has all the components and structure of a persuasive expository essay.[7]

---

identity. The elimination of the monarchy itself would have severely impacted that sense of belonging.

[6] Alma's Argumentative/Persuasive Essays: Alma 5; 7; 9:8-30; 12:12-18,22-37; 13:1-30; 32:16-43; 33:2-23; 36; 37; 38; 40; 41; 42. Descriptive Essay: Alma 29 (Alma's soliloquy). Exposition Essay: Alma 39.

[7] The rhetorical modes of Alma's essays to his three sons are Persuasion (Alma 36-38), Exposition (Alma 39), and Argumentation (Alma 40-42), but their content styles are different: Alma 36, 40-42 are Expository while Alma 37-39 are Parental.

Interestingly, when one looks at Alma's essays to his sons that have the expository content style (Alma 36, 40-42), it appears they were originally instructional texts to help members and missionaries understand the gospel. It seems Alma modified these valuable texts

1. Thesis/Position

If you keep the commandments, you will prosper in the land. (v. 1)

This phrase was a common expression among the Nephites (1 Nephi 4:14; 2 Nephi 1:4; Jarom 1:9; Omni 1:6; Mosiah 1:7; 2:22,31; Alma 9:13; 37:13; 38:1; 48:25; 50:20; Helaman 3:20) and Alma uses it as the thesis that all arguments support.

2. The Frame of Argument

Argument 1

Whoever trusts in God shall be supported in their trials, troubles, and afflictions and shall be lifted up at the last day. (v. 3)

This is Alma's first argument in support of his thesis. He provided seven pieces of evidence to support this argument.

Evidence 1

Do what I do, remember the captivity of our fathers. Our fathers, the Israelites, were in bondage and captivity, and God delivered them [because they trusted God]. (v. 2)

---

for his sons as sacred keepsakes so that they will never forget valuable truths and pass them on to their children. Their content style is significantly different than Alma 37-39's parental style, which is intimate and personal, as only a loving father can write to his sons.

Persuasion Strategy	Argument Type	Evidence Type
Logos	Deduction	Objective

Alma mentioned the captivity of their ancestors and God's deliverance of them. This event was accepted as an indisputable factual event by the Nephites, making it objective evidence from their point of view.

Evidence 2

My knowledge of this truth comes from God. If I have not been born of God, I would not know these things. But God made them known to me by the mouth of his holy angel. (v. 4-5)

Persuasion Strategy	Argument Type	Evidence Type
Ethos	Abduction	Subjective

Alma was transformed (born of God), making him credible; the angel was also trustworthy. Being "born of God" changed him. The evidence that what he is saying about the angel is real is by how he revamped his life, turned away from sin, and strove to follow God no matter what. People can evaluate the subjective evidence indirectly – how he lives his life now compared to how he lived previously. The argument is abductive since being born of God is the simplest explanation for why Alma changed his life and behavior.

Evidence 3

I was struck with such great fear and amazement lest perhaps that I should be destroyed ... I was racked with eternal torment for my soul was harrowed up to the greatest degree and racked with all my sins. I was tormented with the pains of hell because I had rebelled against my God, and that <u>I had not kept his holy commandments</u> (v. 11-13) ... So great had been my iniquities, that the very thought of coming into the presence of my God did rack my soul with inexpressible horror. (v. 14) I wish I could become extinct in both soul and body so that I would not be brought to stand in the presence of my God, to be judged of my deeds (v. 15). I was racked with the pains of a damned soul for three days and three nights. (v. 16)

Persuasion Strategy	Argument Type	Evidence Type
Pathos	Induction	Subjective

Alma is painting a picture of how terrifying it is to be a sinner without forgiveness. He vividly describes his dread at the idea of standing in the presence of God while not keeping his commandments. Extinction is preferable than going into God's presence while still a sinner.

The argument is inductive since the conclusion is likely given the premise. And the evidence is subjective since the audience did not witness what Alma saw.

Evidence 4

While I was in torment and harrowed up by the memory of my sins, I remembered that my father prophesied that one Jesus Christ, a son of God, was going to come to atone for the sins of the world. While my mind caught hold of this thought, I cried within my heart: **"O Jesus, thou Son of God, have mercy on me, who am in the gall of bitterness."** *(v. 17-18) When I thought this, I could remember my pains no more; yea, I was harrowed up by the memory of my sins no more. (v. 19) And oh, what joy, and what marvelous light I did behold; yea, my soul was filled with joy as exceeding as was my pain. There could be nothing so exquisite and so bitter as were my pains and nothing so exquisite and sweet as my joy. (v. 20-21) Methought I saw God sitting upon his throne, surrounded with numberless concourses of angels ... singing and praising their God ... and my soul did long to be there. (v. 22)*

Persuasion Strategy	Argument Type	Evidence Type
Pathos	Induction	Subjective

Alma emphasizes that Christ changes our moral state, from sinful to sinless. When he called upon Christ, his sins and guilt vanished, and he felt incredible joy and yearned to be with God.

Fear, trust, joy, awe, and yearning are all present. The argument is inductive since the conclusion is likely given the premise. The evidence is subjective since the audience did not witness what Alma saw.

Evidence 5
Many have also been born of God and have tasted what I tasted, and have seen as I have seen, and know as I know that the knowledge I have is of God. (v. 26)

Persuasion Strategy	Argument Type	Evidence Type
Logos	Deduction	Objective

Alma points out that other eyewitnesses exist who can confirm that Alma's knowledge is from God because they have experienced what he experienced. This makes the evidence objective despite individually subjective.

Evidence 6
God has consistently delivered me from trials, troubles, and afflictions because I put my trust in him. (v. 27)

Persuasion Strategy	Argument Type	Evidence Type
Logos	Deduction	Objective

Many can confirm that Alma has consistently been delivered from trials, troubles, and afflictions. Alma claims his trust in God has always delivered him.

Evidence 7

And I know that [God] will raise me up at the last day, to dwell with him in glory because he brought our fathers out of bondage and captivity. I have always remembered their captivity, and you should as well. (v. 28-29)

Persuasion Strategy	Argument Type	Evidence Type
Logos	Deduction	Subjective

Alma asserts that he knows God will raise him up on the last day to dwell with him in glory because the Lord delivered their ancestors from bondage. Alma ties in a belief that everyone believes to be real with his central point that Jesus saves. He argues if one is true, then the other is as well.

This means the argument is deductive since the audience knows their ancestors were delivered from bondage (from Egypt and from the Lamanites), but the evidence is subjective since the audience cannot confirm that God will save Alma on the last day.

Argument 2

I am born of God (v. 23)

Part 2: Alma 36's Multifaceted Structure 163

This is Alma's second argument to support his thesis. To be "born of God" means one keeps God's commandments and thus prospers in the land. He provides three pieces of evidence to support this argument.

Evidence 1

From that time until now, I have labored without ceasing that I might bring souls unto repentance so that they may also taste of the same great joy I tasted so that they may also be born of God and be filled with the Holy Spirit. (v. 24)

Persuasion Strategy	Argument Type	Evidence Type
Logos	Deduction	Objective

Alma cites his confirmable actions as evidence that he has been "born of God" (a phrase unique to Alma in the Book of Mormon). It is objective since the audience can confirm that Alma was trying to convert them.

Evidence 2

The Lord gives me great joy in the fruit of my labor. (v. 25)

Persuasion Strategy	Argument Type	Evidence Type
Pathos	Abduction	Subjective

Alma mentions his great pleasure in those who convert or return to Christ. This joy is evidence that he has been born of God.

The argument is abductive since it appears evident that the most likely explanation for why Alma abandoned the comforts of his previous life to preach the Gospel is because he experienced a spiritual transformation. The evidence is subjective because the audience cannot know if the conversion is genuine (they can only believe).

Evidence 3

Many have also been born of God and have tasted what I tasted, and have seen as I have seen, and know as I know that the knowledge I have is of God. (v. 26)

Persuasion Strategy	Argument Type	Evidence Type
Logos	Deduction	Objective

Alma points out that other people exist who can confirm the truth of his claims.

3. Essay Conclusion

You need to know just as I know that provided you keep the commandments of God, you shall prosper in the land. And if you refuse to keep his commandments, you will be cut off from God's presence. (v. 30)

Alma concludes his essay by coming full circle to his thesis.

Thesis Restatement

If you keep the commandments of God, you shall prosper in the land. And if you refuse to keep his commandments, you will be cut off from God's presence. (v. 30)

Call to Action

Remember the bondage and captivity of our fathers, just as I remember them. (v. 29)

Know even as I know that if you keep God's commandments, you will prosper. (v. 30)

Attempt to Modify the Audience's Worldview

Obedience to God's commandments brings unimaginably glorious rewards (v. 30 cf. v. 20-22), while disobedience brings unimaginable horror (v. 30 cf. v. 12-16).

Subsection Summary

Everything Alma does in this chapter is designed to make the audience believe in Christ, convert to him, and keep God's commandments.

Its structure is clearly organized, with two arguments supporting the thesis and multiple evidence pieces supporting each argument. It uses the pathos, ethos, and logos persuasive strategies. Alma's conclusion contains all three types of persuasive essay conclusions: He reiterated the thesis, issued two calls to action, and tried to change the audience's worldview by pointing out that those who keep God's commandments will receive glory beyond description. In contrast, those who do not keep his commandments will receive utter terror.

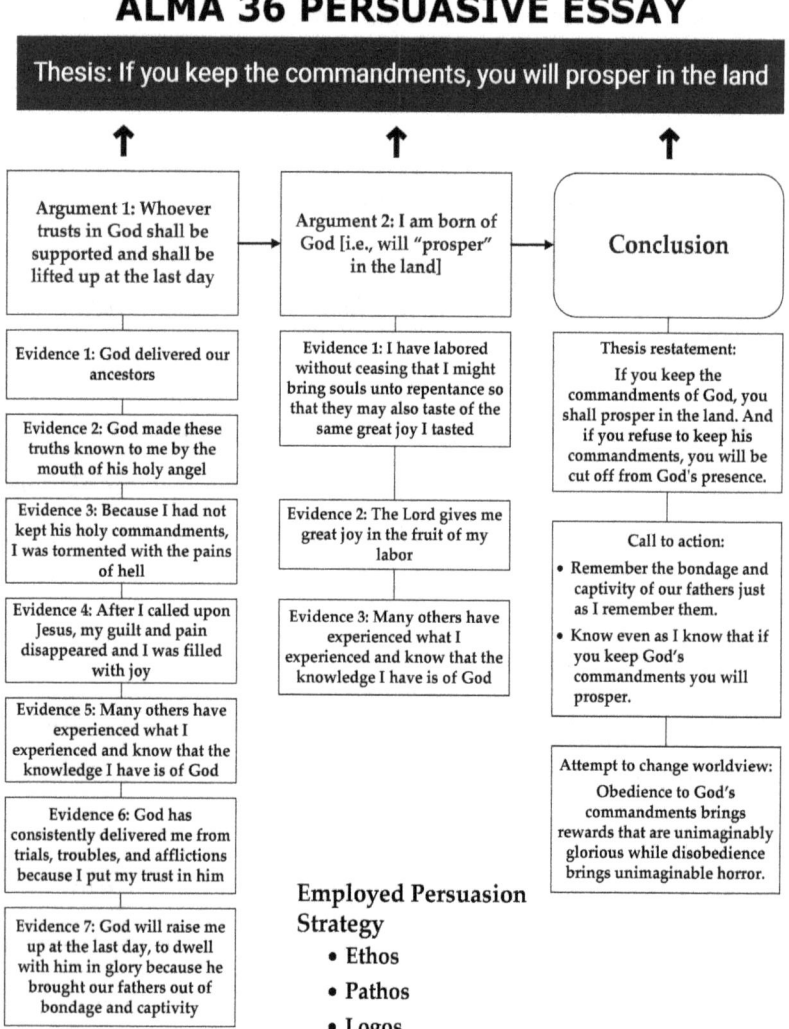

Figure 14: Alma 36's Persuasion Essay Structure

Figure 14 shows that each piece of evidence supports an argument, and each argument supports the thesis. The conclusion also supports the thesis. This demonstrates Alma 36 is a persuasive essay within the audience's worldview, where the belief that God freed their ancestors from captivity is accepted as a fact that everybody knows.

While today's top universities require better arguments and pieces of evidence due to the modern Western worldview, the arguments and pieces of evidence within Alma 36 are credible to the original audience and are structurally valid.

Facet 2: Alma 36 as a Modified Public Speech

Alma was the high priest and former chief judge over the Nephites, which would be roughly analogous to being the prophet of the Church while also being the ex-president of the nation. These roles made Alma the most prominent person in the land.

Since the sons of King Mosiah left to preach to the Lamanites (Mosiah 28:1-10; Alma 17-26), Alma was the only living witness to the angel's appearance. As mentioned above, this pivotal event caused one of the most significant changes to the Nephite society in five centuries: the monarchy was abolished, people were given new rights and responsibilities, and the central government was weakened to such an extent that entire provinces essentially became autonomous.

As typical humans, it is likely that the Nephites would have wanted to know about the supernatural event that upended their world and gave them much greater self-rule. If so, then it is possible that a common request they would have asked Alma was:

"*Tell us about the angel!*"

Alma had a fantastic story to tell, and he knew it. And it is fair to presume that most of those he encountered would have wanted to hear it – Alma even related his version of the conversion event to the people of Anti-Nephi-Lehi the first time they met him (Alma 27:25) even though they lived with the other four witnesses for years.

Since this missionary-minded man knew the public would have wanted to make sense of the change they experienced, it makes sense that he would have used the supernatural event to help convince people to believe in and stay faithful to Christ.[8]

There is no doubt that Alma was intelligent and driven to succeed. Would he be like the most successful preachers, those who solidify their thoughts by writing

---

[8] Alma uses words and phrases that tie into the angel's appearance in Alma 5, 7, 9-13, 29, 30, 32-33, 38-42. See Brown, S. K.

them down and refining them, or would he just wing it and speak without preparation and organization?

When putting it this way, it becomes likely that Alma would have been just like professional speakers today. He would have written down and improved his speeches before he gave them. If providing the same address to different audiences, then he would have tweaked them based on lessons learned and on what he knew of the new audience (e.g., "I'm so happy to be speaking to the best pottery craftsmen in the nation, the great and wonderful people of the city of Aaron!").

Given the angel's appearance not only changed Nephite society but also changed Alma into a follower of Jesus Christ, it is reasonable to assume he wrote down his conversion story, which he would then read out to crowds in the hopes that they, too, would become disciples of Christ. And what better conversion story could he make than Alma 36?

Alma 36 is likely a modified public speech because it is structurally efficient – it harmonizes cultural baseline beliefs[9] with a personal account[10] within the context of the

---

[9] The common knowledge that the Nephites believed or "knew" to be true.

[10] The personal highlights that occurred to Alma that the public does not necessarily know.

angel's appearance while centered on a specific goal – to bring people to Christ. It works equally well when addressed to just one person or an audience of thousands. While the Book of Mormon never states that it started off as a public speech (after all, it is possible that he just wrote it for his son), the ease of conversion to a highly-effective public speech lends more weight to it starting off as a public-facing conversion story that was later modified for Helaman.

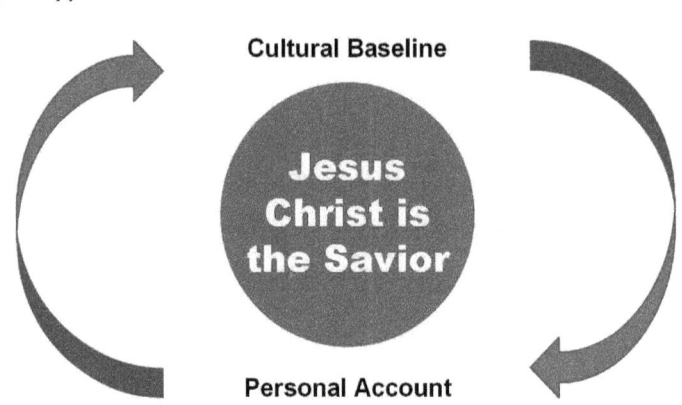

Figure 15: Alma 36's Efficient Structure

The angel's appearance and its effect on the Nephites gave Alma the perfect *hook* to further his goal, and it is unlikely that he would ignore the most effective device in his toolbox for two decades. Since Alma's ministry lasted anywhere from 18-26 years, it is doubtful that all he ever said about the angel's appearance is found in the several

Part 2: Alma 36's Multifaceted Structure 171

hours of preaching recorded in the Book of Mormon. It is absurd to imagine that a person wanting to convert others to Christ would not have capitalized on his conversion story and would wait until the end of his life before writing it down and then merely give it to his son, Helaman, instead of telling the people directly.

If Alma 36 was originally a public speech, then Alma simply changed one word six times ("brethren" to "son") and added nine words in the third verse to give Helaman a personalized copy.

Table 2: Side-by-Side Comparison of the Public Speech Version and the Personalized Version of Alma 36

Alma 36	
Public Speech Version	**Personalized Version**
My **brethren**, give ear to my words; for I swear unto you, that inasmuch as ye shall keep the commandments of God ye shall prosper in the land. I would that ye should do as I have done, in remembering the captivity of our fathers; for they were in bondage, and none could deliver them except it was the God of Abraham, and the God of Isaac, and the	My **son**, give ear to my words; for I swear unto you, that inasmuch as ye shall keep the commandments of God ye shall prosper in the land. I would that ye should do as I have done, in remembering the captivity of our fathers; for they were in bondage, and none could deliver them except it was the God of Abraham, and the God of Isaac, and the

Alma 36	
Public Speech Version	**Personalized Version**
God of Jacob; and he surely did deliver them in their afflictions. And now, O my **brethren**,	God of Jacob; and he surely did deliver them in their afflictions. And now, O my **son Helaman, behold, thou art in thy youth, and therefore,**
I beseech of thee that thou wilt hear my words and learn of me; for I do know that whosoever shall put their trust in God shall be supported in their trials, and their troubles, and their afflictions, and shall be lifted up at the last day. And I would not that ye think that I know of myself—not of the temporal but of the spiritual, not of the carnal mind but of God. Now, behold, I say unto you, if I had not been born of God I should not have known these things; but God has, by the mouth of his holy angel, made these things known unto me, not of any worthiness of myself.	I beseech of thee that thou wilt hear my words and learn of me; for I do know that whosoever shall put their trust in God shall be supported in their trials, and their troubles, and their afflictions, and shall be lifted up at the last day. And I would not that ye think that I know of myself—not of the temporal but of the spiritual, not of the carnal mind but of God. Now, behold, I say unto you, if I had not been born of God I should not have known these things; but God has, by the mouth of his holy angel, made these things known unto me, not of any worthiness of myself.

Alma 36

Public Speech Version	Personalized Version
For I went about with the sons of Mosiah, seeking to destroy the church of God; but behold, God sent his holy angel to stop us by the way. And behold, he spake unto us, as it were the voice of thunder, and the whole earth did tremble beneath our feet; and we all fell to the earth, for the fear of the Lord came upon us. But behold, the voice said unto me: Arise. And I arose and stood up, and beheld the angel. And he said unto me: If thou wilt of thyself be destroyed, seek no more to destroy the church of God. And it came to pass that I fell to the earth; and it was for the space of three days and three nights that I could not open my mouth, neither had I the use of my limbs. And the angel spake more things unto me, which were heard by my brethren, but I did not hear them; for when I	For I went about with the sons of Mosiah, seeking to destroy the church of God; but behold, God sent his holy angel to stop us by the way. And behold, he spake unto us, as it were the voice of thunder, and the whole earth did tremble beneath our feet; and we all fell to the earth, for the fear of the Lord came upon us. But behold, the voice said unto me: Arise. And I arose and stood up, and beheld the angel. And he said unto me: If thou wilt of thyself be destroyed, seek no more to destroy the church of God. And it came to pass that I fell to the earth; and it was for the space of three days and three nights that I could not open my mouth, neither had I the use of my limbs. And the angel spake more things unto me, which were heard by my brethren, but I did not hear them; for when I

Alma 36	
Public Speech Version	**Personalized Version**
heard the words—If thou wilt be destroyed of thyself, seek no more to destroy the church of God—I was struck with such great fear and amazement lest perhaps I should be destroyed, that I fell to the earth and I did hear no more. But I was racked with eternal torment, for my soul was harrowed up to the greatest degree and racked with all my sins. Yea, I did remember all my sins and iniquities, for which I was tormented with the pains of hell; yea, I saw that I had rebelled against my God, and that I had not kept his holy commandments. Yea, and I had murdered many of his children, or rather led them away unto destruction; yea, and in fine so great had been my iniquities, that the very thought of coming into the presence of my God did	heard the words—If thou wilt be destroyed of thyself, seek no more to destroy the church of God—I was struck with such great fear and amazement lest perhaps I should be destroyed, that I fell to the earth and I did hear no more. But I was racked with eternal torment, for my soul was harrowed up to the greatest degree and racked with all my sins. Yea, I did remember all my sins and iniquities, for which I was tormented with the pains of hell; yea, I saw that I had rebelled against my God, and that I had not kept his holy commandments. Yea, and I had murdered many of his children, or rather led them away unto destruction; yea, and in fine so great had been my iniquities, that the very thought of coming into the presence of my God did

Alma 36	
Public Speech Version	**Personalized Version**
rack my soul with inexpressible horror. Oh, thought I, that I could be banished and become extinct both soul and body, that I might not be brought to stand in the presence of my God, to be judged of my deeds. And now, for three days and for three nights was I racked, even with the pains of a damned soul. And it came to pass that as I was thus racked with torment, while I was harrowed up by the memory of my many sins – behold, I remembered also to have heard my father prophesy unto the people concerning the coming of one Jesus Christ, a Son of God, to atone for the sins of the world. Now, as my mind caught hold upon this thought, I cried within my heart: O Jesus, thou Son of God, have mercy on me, who am in the gall of bitterness, and am encircled	rack my soul with inexpressible horror. Oh, thought I, that I could be banished and become extinct both soul and body, that I might not be brought to stand in the presence of my God, to be judged of my deeds. And now, for three days and for three nights was I racked, even with the pains of a damned soul. And it came to pass that as I was thus racked with torment, while I was harrowed up by the memory of my many sins – behold, I remembered also to have heard my father prophesy unto the people concerning the coming of one Jesus Christ, a Son of God, to atone for the sins of the world. Now, as my mind caught hold upon this thought, I cried within my heart: O Jesus, thou Son of God, have mercy on me, who am in the gall of bitterness, and am encircled

Alma 36	
Public Speech Version	**Personalized Version**
about by the everlasting chains of death. And now, behold, when I thought this, I could remember my pains no more; yea, I was harrowed up by the memory of my sins no more. And oh, what joy, and what marvelous light I did behold; yea, my soul was filled with joy as exceeding as was my pain! Yea, I say unto you, my **brethren**, that there could be nothing so exquisite and so bitter as were my pains. Yea, and again I say unto you, my **brethren**, that on the other hand, there can be nothing so exquisite and sweet as was my joy. Yea, methought I saw, even as our father Lehi saw, God sitting upon his throne, surrounded with numberless concourses of angels, in the attitude of singing and praising their God; yea, and my soul did long to be there.	about by the everlasting chains of death. And now, behold, when I thought this, I could remember my pains no more; yea, I was harrowed up by the memory of my sins no more. And oh, what joy, and what marvelous light I did behold; yea, my soul was filled with joy as exceeding as was my pain! Yea, I say unto you, my **son**, that there could be nothing so exquisite and so bitter as were my pains. Yea, and again I say unto you, my **son**, that on the other hand, there can be nothing so exquisite and sweet as was my joy. Yea, methought I saw, even as our father Lehi saw, God sitting upon his throne, surrounded with numberless concourses of angels, in the attitude of singing and praising their God; yea, and my soul did long to be there.

Part 2: Alma 36's Multifaceted Structure

Alma 36	
Public Speech Version	**Personalized Version**
But behold, my limbs did receive their strength again, and I stood upon my feet, and did manifest unto the people that I had been born of God. Yea, and from that time even until now, I have labored without ceasing, that I might bring souls unto repentance; that I might bring them to taste of the exceeding joy of which I did taste; that they might also be born of God, and be filled with the Holy Ghost. Yea, and now behold, O my **brethren**, the Lord doth give me exceedingly great joy in the fruit of my labors; For because of the word which he has imparted unto me, behold, many have been born of God, and have tasted as I have tasted, and have seen eye to eye as I have seen; therefore they do know of these things of which I have spoken, as I do know; and the knowledge which I have is of God. And I	But behold, my limbs did receive their strength again, and I stood upon my feet, and did manifest unto the people that I had been born of God. Yea, and from that time even until now, I have labored without ceasing, that I might bring souls unto repentance; that I might bring them to taste of the exceeding joy of which I did taste; that they might also be born of God, and be filled with the Holy Ghost. Yea, and now behold, O my **son**, the Lord doth give me exceedingly great joy in the fruit of my labors; For because of the word which he has imparted unto me, behold, many have been born of God, and have tasted as I have tasted, and have seen eye to eye as I have seen; therefore they do know of these things of which I have spoken, as I do know; and the knowledge which I have is of God. And I

Alma 36	
Public Speech Version	**Personalized Version**
have been supported under trials and troubles of every kind, yea, and in all manner of afflictions; yea, God has delivered me from prison, and from bonds, and from death; yea, and I do put my trust in him, and he will still deliver me. And I know that he will raise me up at the last day, to dwell with him in glory; yea, and I will praise him forever. For he has brought our fathers out of Egypt, and he has swallowed up the Egyptians in the Red Sea; and he led them by his power into the promised land; yea, and he has delivered them out of bondage and captivity from time to time. Yea, and he has also brought our fathers out of the land of Jerusalem; and he has also, by his everlasting power, delivered them out of bondage and captivity, from time to time even down to the	have been supported under trials and troubles of every kind, yea, and in all manner of afflictions; yea, God has delivered me from prison, and from bonds, and from death; yea, and I do put my trust in him, and he will still deliver me. And I know that he will raise me up at the last day, to dwell with him in glory; yea, and I will praise him forever. For he has brought our fathers out of Egypt, and he has swallowed up the Egyptians in the Red Sea; and he led them by his power into the promised land; yea, and he has delivered them out of bondage and captivity from time to time. Yea, and he has also brought our fathers out of the land of Jerusalem; and he has also, by his everlasting power, delivered them out of bondage and captivity, from time to time even down to the

Alma 36	
Public Speech Version	**Personalized Version**
present day; and I have always retained in remembrance their captivity; yea, and ye also ought to retain in remembrance, as I have done, their captivity. But behold, my **brethren**, this is not all; for ye ought to know as I do know, that inasmuch as ye shall keep the commandments of God ye shall prosper in the land; and ye ought to know also, that inasmuch as ye will not keep the commandments of God ye shall be cut off from his presence. Now this is according to his word.	present day; and I have always retained in remembrance their captivity; yea, and ye also ought to retain in remembrance, as I have done, their captivity. But behold, my **son**, this is not all; for ye ought to know as I do know, that inasmuch as ye shall keep the commandments of God ye shall prosper in the land; and ye ought to know also, that inasmuch as ye will not keep the commandments of God ye shall be cut off from his presence. Now this is according to his word.

Reading the public speech version aloud shows a conversion story that can effectively influence its listeners.[11] This explains why it is a persuasive essay instead of an argumentative essay. This also explains why it is structurally a chiasm.

---

[11] The word "brethren" would have been used instead of "people" to be consistent with Alma's usage.

While it may seem strange to those in our culture to have a father give his son a personalized copy of his conversion speech,[12] this is no more unlikely than a parent giving his child an autographed copy of his book. And as to why only to Helaman and not his other sons – we have no way of knowing, but an attractive assumption is that it was given as a "double-blessing" following the ancient Israelite practice for their firstborn son (cf. Deuteronomy 21:17).[13]

Facet 3: Alma 36 as a Thematic Chiasm

"A chiasm is a balanced grammatical structure where words, phrases, or ideas (themes) are repeated, often roughly or sometimes precisely in reverse order after a central point."[14]

---

[12] Interestingly, the Alma 40-42 block appears to be three doctrinal lessons that Alma modified for Corianton.

[13] Welch, J. W. (1991). p. 130.

[14] Per Stephen Ehat (in personal correspondence with this author). Also, "The characteristics of balance and symmetry differ in the analysis of chiastic and other parallelistic structures. 'Balance' refers to the appearance in the second flank (second half) of a proposed chiasm in a lengthy text of words, phrases, or ideas (concepts) already stated earlier in the first flank (or half) of that text. 'Symmetry' in that analysis is the quality of an exact or sometimes inexact reversal in the sequence of the repetition of the elements—the words, phrases, or ideas (concepts). Asymmetry (a lack of symmetry or lack of complete symmetry), at least to some extent, is not only

Ever since John W. Welch[15] discovered chiasmus in the Book of Mormon in 1967,[16] it has been cited as evidence of its authenticity. Computer models show a 99.98% certainty that the chiastic structure of Alma 36 was done intentionally.[17]

Recognizing Alma 36 as a public speech explains the presence of chiasmus within the document because it is a memory aid to help listeners retain the core message.[18]

Keyword/Phrase Chiastic Models and Their Problems

One can sense Alma 36's chiasmus whenever reading or hearing it, but mapping it out has been problematic since it can be mapped out as an eight-element model,[19] nine-

---

often observed in chiasms but even seemingly preferred in Hebrew texts, as some scholars note, so as to avoid violation of the Second Commandment of the Decalogue."

[15] John ("Jack") W. Welch provided invaluable help in making this book better. His insight and encyclopedic knowledge of all things chiasmus are a joy to experience.

[16] Welch, J. W. (2007). p.75.

[17] Edwards, B. F., Edwards, W. F. p. 123.

[18] Chiasmus appears in ancient literature across the world. Most notably, it is found throughout the Holy Bible and the Book of Mormon. See Chiasmus Resources.

[19] Edwards, B. F., Edwards, W. F. p. 121.

element model,[20] ten-element model,[21] eleven-element model,[22] fifteen-element model,[23] and even a seventeen-element model.[24]

The confusion as to which model is legitimate lies in the usage of paired keywords and phrases. While the more significant number of paired words and concepts are more impressive evidence of deliberate creation, using them exacerbates the charge of cherry-picking or confirmation bias because of the number of words and ideas that are ignored to make the chiasmus work.[25] The larger models also break up clauses and ignore out-of-sequence elements.

The smaller models are structurally sounder than the larger models but leave too much text outside the structure. The seventeen-element model is the most visually impressive but is also the most vulnerable to the cherry-picking charge by those who ignore the asymmetry common to many if not most large chiasms in ancient literature.

---

[20] Reynolds, N. B. p. 6, 14-39.

[21] Edwards, B. F., Edwards, W. F. p. 121.

[22] Welch, J. W. (1970) p. 83.

[23] FAIR.

[24] Welch, J. W. (1991) p. 114-131.

[25] Wunderli, E. M. p. 97-110.

This book sidesteps the entire issue of symmetry vs. asymmetry of word and phrase chiasmus by pointing out that Alma 36 is definitely a chiasm but not one driven by keywords or phrases. It is actually a thematic chiasm that encompasses every single word of the chapter, making it immune to the cherry-picking charge. And the matching words and phrases, while important, are secondary to the partnered themes.

Thematic Chiasm Model

When one places themselves in Alma's shoes as someone who wants to use his conversion story to convince people to believe in Christ, it then becomes easy to see Alma outlining his persuasive speech and refining it after each retelling –like any good public speaker today. His desire to succeed would result in writing his conversion story according to the anticipated comprehensibility of his audience, who would have been used to receiving information by oral transmission. Being a missionary-minded man, he would not use abstract ideas for themes; he would use items directly relevant to his audience.

By thinking of Alma's mindset and his audience's capability, he would most likely create a structure that is complex enough to be impressive but small enough that those used to oral transmission of knowledge can remember the highlights. And he would use repetition such as a forward and backward pass of the same points for memory retention, which explains the layout. Thus, the most likely chiastic model in Alma 36 is a seven-element model using specific themes that he would have outlined beforehand:

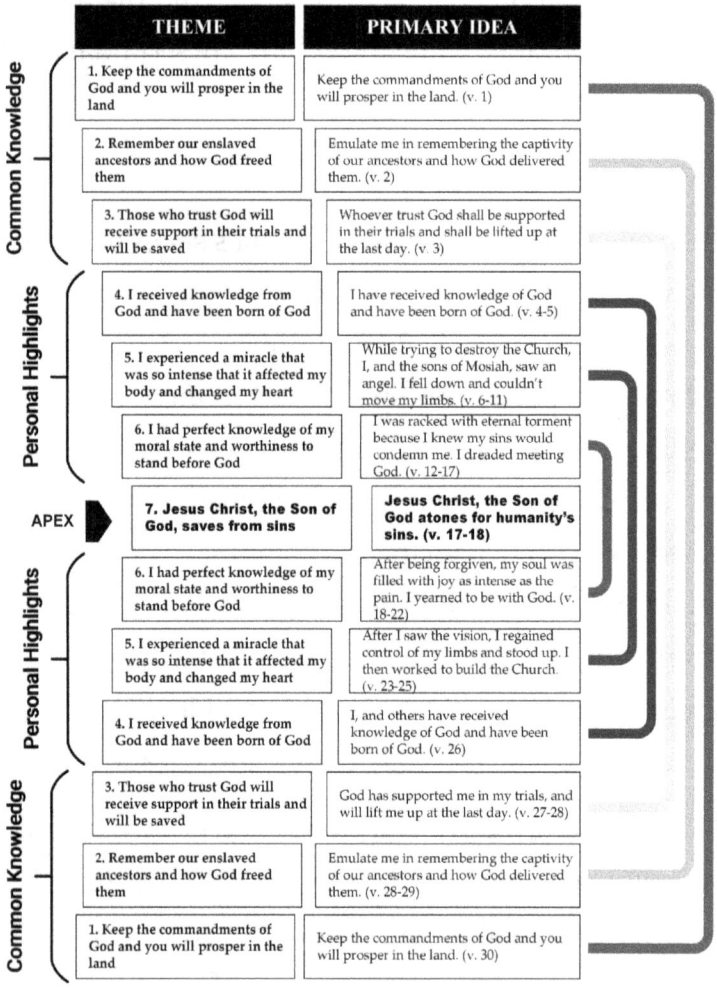

Figure 16: Alma 36's Chiastic Structure Based on Primary Themes

The themes would be laid out in an organized manner where one theme progresses to the next. After the apex is reached, the themes are revisited in reverse order:

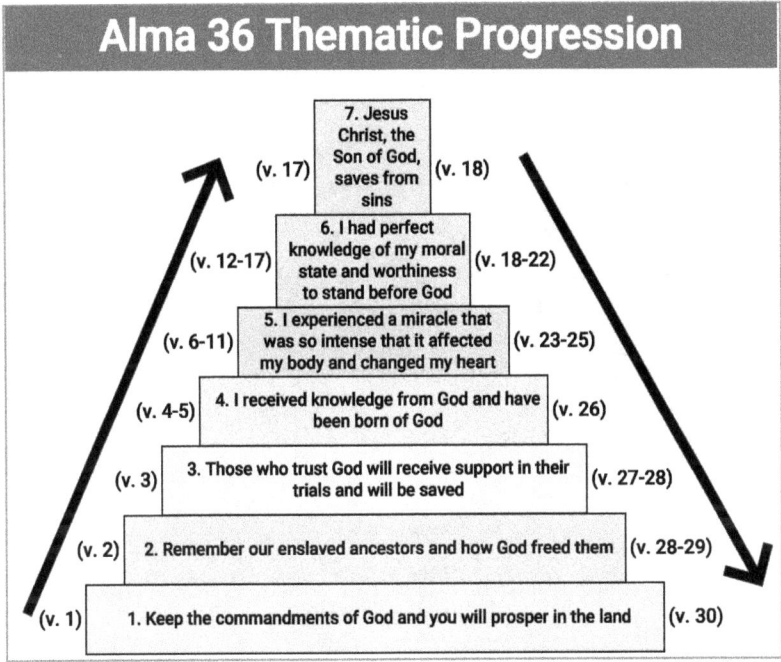

Figure 17: Alma 36 Thematic Progression

Alma moves from theme to theme, step-by-step, as if he is climbing up and down a mountain. Crucial key words and phrases are repeated within the theme for memory retention, but their sequence within the theme is not Alma's main priority—the themes are.

Another way of looking at the chiasm would be to employ a concentric model (Figure 18) to show Alma 36's intentional design.

186   Verifiable Evidence for the Book of Mormon

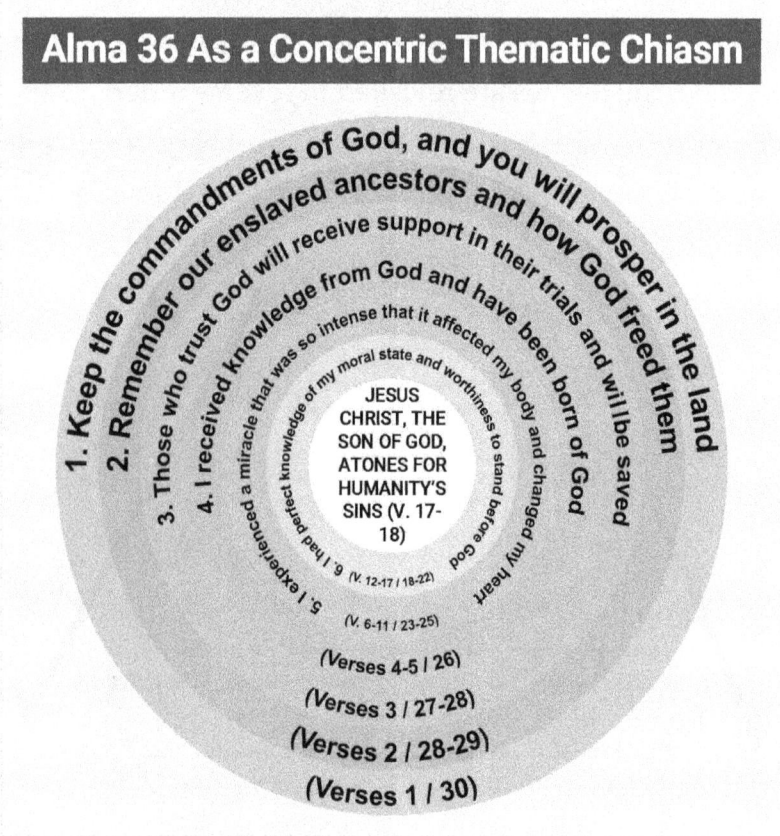

Figure 18: Alma 36's Thematic Chiasm Using the Concentric Model

Using a seven-element model according to the above themes covers the entire chapter and does not overlook any piece or split clauses. There is no need to force the chiasm to accept single words or skip over thoughts that do not fit the desired structure. It does not jump over ideas that are out of place in other models. It is simple enough for people to remember Alma's most essential points while preserving the chiasm.

But what is important to note is the keywords/phrases do *not* need to be a chiasmus between themselves; they only need to be grouped *within the same theme*.

The first three themes are comprised of shared knowledge – the Nephite cultural baseline of beliefs that Alma's audience already knew and agreed with since that is what they were taught all their lives:

1. Keep the commandments of God, and you will prosper in the land.

This theme is found throughout the Book of Mormon (1 Nephi 4:14; 2 Nephi 1:4; Jarom 1:9; Omni 1:6; Mosiah 1:7; 2:22,31; Alma 9:13; 37:13; 38:1; 48:25; 50:20; Helaman 3:20) and shows the expression was part of their culture just as "Choose the right" is part of the modern Church's culture.

2. Remember our enslaved ancestors and how God freed them.

The Book of Mormon has numerous passages where the people are told to remember the captivity of their ancestors and how God delivered them from bondage. Those who were delivered were the Israelites from Egypt (1 Nephi 4:2-3; 17:23-27; 19:10; Mosiah 7:19-20; 12:34) and the people of Limhi who reintegrated into the Nephites (Mosiah 7:15,22,33; Mosiah 23:23-24; 24:13-17,21; 29:18-20). Lehi's departure from Jerusalem was also viewed as God delivering them from bondage because they avoided the Babylonian conquest and enslavement of the Jews (2 Nephi 1:4; Alma 9:22).

When the angel appeared to Alma, he told him: *"Now I say unto thee: Go, and remember the captivity of thy fathers in the land of Helam, and in the land of Nephi; and remember how great things he has done for them; for they were in bondage, and he has delivered them."* (Mosiah 27:16)

Alma's father, who is also named Alma, *"[exhorted] the people of Limhi and his brethren, all those that had been delivered out of bondage, that they should remember that it was the Lord that did deliver them."* (Mosiah 25:15-16)

Alma took these examples to heart and repeated them several times outside Alma 36 (Alma 5:5-6; 29:11-12).

3. Those who trust God will receive support in their trials and will be saved.

While there is not a lot of textual support in the Book of Mormon for the paired "Trust in God – he will support us" or "Trust in God – he will lift up/save us" (2 Nephi 4:19-20; Mosiah 23:22; Alma 5:13; 38:5) the overall idea is universal and would be familiar to Alma's audience. No one would disagree that those who trust in God will find support in their trials, troubles, and afflictions and will be lifted up on the last day.

> In using the "Common Knowledge" themes that his audience already knew and agreed on, Alma did what

> any good preacher or salesperson does – get them to agree early on before attempting to convert them.

The following three themes are Alma's account of event highlights – those items he wants to talk about that the audience does not yet necessarily know.

4. I received knowledge from God and have been born of God.

Alma claims he has information that they must know and coins a word unique to him in the Book of Mormon: "born of God."

5. I experienced a miracle that was so intense that it affected my body and changed my heart.

The angel's appearance caused Alma to become paralyzed for three days and three nights. But it also did something else.

Before his conversion, Alma was described as:

A man of many words, and did speak much flattery to the people; therefore he led many of the people to do after the manner of his iniquities. And he became a great hinderment to the prosperity of the church of God; stealing away the hearts of the people; causing much dissension among the people; giving a chance for the enemy of God to exercise his power over them. And now it came to pass that while he was going about to destroy the church of God, for he did go about secretly with the sons of Mosiah seeking to destroy the church, and to lead astray the people of the Lord, contrary to the commandments of God, or even the king. (Mosiah 27:8-10)

People like this are charismatic, proud, and arrogant. But when the angel appeared and told him he was doomed, that, in his own words, *"I was struck with such great fear and amazement lest perhaps I should be destroyed, that I fell to the earth and I did hear no more."* (Alma 36:11) Dread filled Alma's heart. He could no longer pretend or imagine that he was right and smarter than his father – the one responsible for organizing the church, who had an actual angel of God on his side!

When he regained the ability to move, he proclaimed his vision and repentance. Alma and the sons of Mosiah then *"began from this time forward to teach the people, and those who were with Alma at the time the angel appeared unto them, traveling round about through all the land, publishing to all the people the things which they had heard and seen, and preaching the word of God."* (Mosiah 27:32) Lastly, *"And they traveled throughout all the land of Zarahemla, and among all the people who were under the reign of king Mosiah, zealously striving to repair all the injuries which they had done to the church, confessing all their sins, and publishing all the things which they had seen."* (Mosiah 27:35)

Alma's attitude reversed due to the angel's appearance.

6. I had perfect knowledge of my moral state and worthiness to stand before God.

Alma experienced the pain and terror of those who die in their sins. The dread at the idea of standing before God while still a sinner was so intense that he wanted to be snuffed out from existence. After Christ forgave him, he experienced the bliss of the saved and now longed to be with God.

7. Jesus Christ, the Son of God, atones for humanity's sins.

The heart of the thematic chiasm is centered on Jesus Christ, the Son of God.

The Themes Frame Alma 36, not Keywords

While keywords may function as memory aids, it is the themes that frame the entire conversion story:

1. *Keep the commandments of God, and you will prosper in the land. (v. 1)*

2. *Remember our enslaved ancestors and how God freed them. (v. 2)*

3. *Those who trust God will receive support in their trials and will be saved. (v. 3)*

4. *I received knowledge from God and have been born of God. (v. 4-5)*

5. *I experienced a miracle that was so intense that it affected my body and changed my heart. (v. 6-11)*

> 6. I had perfect knowledge of my moral state and worthiness to stand before God. (v. 12-17)
>
> **7. Jesus Christ, the Son of God, atones for humanity's sins. (v. 17-18)**
>
> 6. I had perfect knowledge of my moral state and worthiness to stand before God. (v. 19-22)
>
> 5. I experienced a miracle that was so intense that it affected my body and changed my heart. (v. 23-25)
>
> 4. I received knowledge from God and have been born of God. (v. 26)[26]
>
> 3. Those who trust God will receive support in their trials and will be saved. (v. 27-28)
>
> 2. Remember our enslaved ancestors and how God freed them. (v. 28-29)
>
> 1. Keep the commandments of God, and you will prosper in the land. (v. 30)

---

[26] Note: "4. I received knowledge from God and have been born of God (v.26)" does not have Alma repeating he is "born of God." What it says is, "Many have been born of God, and have tasted as I have tasted, and have seen eye to eye as I have seen." So, whatever made these people "born of God" is because they experienced the same thing Alma did. Thus, if A = "born of God" in v.5 and B = "born of God" in v.26, then A = B. The theme label is accurate in both spots since the chiasmus criterion is the theme, not the keyword.

Using a seven-element chiasmus comprised of themes instead of keywords and phrases eliminates the charge of confirmation bias and does not split lines of thought. It follows the outlining process all successful public speakers use to make their speeches effective.

Restricting the themes to just seven and then repeating them in reverse order allows the audience to remember the most important components. This "forward and backward pass" helps people retain information. <u>Even better, Alma's audience already knew the first three!</u> And as the apex or pivot point on Christ is unforgettable, this means they only need to strain to remember three points:

1. Alma, the most famous and prominent man in the nation, received knowledge of God and was born of God.

2. The miraculous angelic appearance affected him deeply on a physical and emotional level.

3. He obtained knowledge of his morality and worthiness before God.

That is it! And the three themes themselves are easily memorable from what one would know about Alma.

Consequently, the thematic chiastic structure is adequate to make an audience member remember Alma's message and the importance of conversion to Christ.

Chiastic Words and Phrases

Alma 36's paired themes drive the placement of the paired or paralleled words and phrases. The themes also frame the content of the unpaired words and phrases. This explains why _all_ words and phrases, both paired and unpaired, snugly fit _within_ each theme.[27]

Table 3: Paired and Unpaired Text Within the Alma 36 Themes

Theme	Verses	Paired/ Paralleled Words and Phrases	Unpaired Words and Phrases
1. Keep the commandments of God, and you will prosper in the land	1 / 30	a. inasmuch as ye keep the commandments of God ye shall prosper in the land / inasmuch as ye shall keep the commandments of God ye shall	/ cut off from [God's] presence / know as I do know

---

[27] Note: The text on the left of the forward slash (/) in Table 3 are the text in the verses before the verse 17/18 divider (i.e., those in verses 1-17) and those to the right of the forward slash are their counterpoints in verses 18-30.

Theme	Verses	Paired/Paralleled Words and Phrases	Unpaired Words and Phrases
		prosper in the land	
2. Remember our enslaved ancestors and how God freed them	2 / 28-29	b. remembering the captivity / I have always retained in remembrance their captivity c. [God] surely did deliver them / [God] has delivered them	do as I have done/ /swallowed up the Egyptians in the Red Sea / [God] led them by his power into the promised land / [God] brought our fathers out of the land of Jerusalem
3. Those who trust God will receive support in their trials and will be saved	3 / 27-28	d. Trust in God / I do put my trust in [God] e. Supported in their trials, and their troubles, and their afflictions / supported under	/ I beseech of thee that thou wilt hear my words and learn of me; for I do know / God has delivered me from prisons,

Theme	Verses	Paired/ Paralleled Words and Phrases	Unpaired Words and Phrases
		trials, and troubles of every kind, yea, and in all manner of afflictions f. [I] shall be lifted up at the last day / [God] will raise me up at the last day	and from bonds, and from death / [God] will still deliver me / to dwell with [God] in glory / I will praise him forever
4. I received knowledge from God and have been born of God	4-5 / 26	g. I know of myself ... not of the carnal mind but of God / as I do know; and the knowledge which I have is of God h. born of God / born of God	By the mouth of his holy angel / Not of any worthiness of myself / / Yea, and from that time even until now, I have labored without ceasing, that I might bring souls unto repentance; that I might bring them to taste of

Part 2: Alma 36's Multifaceted Structure   197

Theme	Verses	Paired/ Paralleled Words and Phrases	Unpaired Words and Phrases
			the exceeding joy of which I did taste
			/ and be filled with the Holy Ghost
			/ have tasted as I have tasted, and have seen eye to eye as I have seen; therefore they do know of these things of which I have spoken
5. I experienced a miracle that was so intense that it affected my body and changed my heart	6-11 / 23-25	i. For I went about with the sons of Mosiah, seeking to destroy the church of God / Yea, and from that time even until now, I have labored without	But behold, God sent his holy angel to stop us by the way. And behold, he spake unto us, as it were the voice of thunder, and the whole earth did tremble

Theme	Verses	Paired/ Paralleled Words and Phrases	Unpaired Words and Phrases
		ceasing, that I might bring souls unto repentance; that I might bring them to taste of the exceeding joy of which I did taste; that they might also be born of God, and be filled with the Holy Ghost j. I fell to the earth; and it was for the space of three days and three nights that I could not open my mouth, neither had I the use of my limbs / [after three days and nights] my limbs did	beneath our feet / the fear of the Lord came upon us / but behold, the voice said unto me: Arise. And I arose and stood up / and he said unto me: If thou wilt of thyself be destroyed / And the angel spake more things unto me, which were heard by my brethren, but I did not hear them; for when I heard the words—If thou wilt be

Part 2: Alma 36's Multifaceted Structure   199

Theme	Verses	Paired/Paralleled Words and Phrases	Unpaired Words and Phrases
		receive their strength again, and stood upon my feet	destroyed of thyself / —I was struck with such great fear and amazement lest perhaps I should be destroyed /
			/ the Lord doth give me exceedingly great joy in the fruit of my labors; for because of the word which he has imparted unto me
6. I had perfect knowledge of my moral state and worthiness to stand before God	12-17 / 18-22	k. I was racked with eternal torment, for my soul was harrowed up to the greatest degree and racked with all my sins ... I was	I saw that I had rebelled against my God, and that I had not kept his holy commandments. I had murdered many of his children, or

Theme	Verses	Paired/ Paralleled Words and Phrases	Unpaired Words and Phrases
		tormented with the pains of hell / who am in the gall of bitterness and am encircled about by the everlasting chains of death. And now, behold, when I thought this, I could remember my pains no more … my soul was filled with joy as exceeding as was my pain! … there could be nothing so exquisite and so bitter as was my pains … there can be nothing so exquisite and	rather led them away unto destruction / And now, for three days and for three nights was I racked, even with the pains of a damned soul. / / what joy, and what marvelous light I did behold / Yea, and methought I saw, even as our father Lehi saw, God sitting upon his throne, surrounded with numberless concourses of angels, in the attitude of singing and

Theme	Verses	Paired/ Paralleled Words and Phrases	Unpaired Words and Phrases
		sweet as was my joy	praising their God
		l. I did remember all my sins and iniquities / I was harrowed up by the memory of my sins no more	
		m. The very thoughts of coming into the presence of my God did rack my soul with inexpressible horror. Oh, thought I, that I could be banished and become extinct both soul and body, that I might not be brought to stand in the presence	

Theme	Verses	Paired/ Paralleled Words and Phrases	Unpaired Words and Phrases
		of my God, to be judged of my deeds. / [after being forgiven,] my soul did long to be [in God's presence]	
7. Jesus Christ, the Son of God, saves from sins	17-18	n. Jesus Christ, a Son of God / O Jesus, thou Son of God	To atone for the sins of the world/ / have mercy on me

As shown above, all unpaired words and phrases are related to the themes where they are located. For example, the unpaired *"do as I have done"* in v. 2 and v. 28-29's *"swallowed up the Egyptians in the Red Sea"*; *"[God] led them by his power into the promised land"*; and *"[God] brought our fathers out of the land of Jerusalem"* fit within Theme 2's *"Remember our enslaved ancestors and how God freed them."* The v. 2's *"do as I have done"* is about remembering the enslaved ancestors, and the v. 28-29's three unpaired phrases are all about the deliverance of these ancestors.

Another example would be the "destroy the Church" passages found inside Theme 5 *"I experienced a miracle that was so intense that it affected my body and changed my heart"* (v. 6-11/23-24). The matching passages are in v. 6 and 24 but v. 9 and 11 are unpaired since the point of the concept elements within that theme was not the attempt to destroy the Church per se on the one hand and build it up on the other, but to illustrate what happened to Alma's body and mindset. The miracle utterly changed him.

These are not coincidences.

Each theme accurately encloses both the paired elements and the unpaired ones.

Types of Pairings

Alma 36 contains 14 conceptual pairings (a-n) within the seven themes. The pairings are mostly repetitions, but some are reversals:

Table 4: Alma 36 Conceptual Pairings and Types

No.	Point	Counterpoint	Type
a	Keep the commandments of God, and ye shall prosper in the land (v. 1)	Keep the commandments of God, and ye shall prosper in the land (v. 30)	Repetition

No.	Point	Counterpoint	Type
b	Remember the captivity of our ancestors (v. 2)	I always remember the captivity of our ancestors (v. 29)	Repetition
c	[God] surely did deliver them (v. 2)	[God] has delivered them (v. 28)	Repetition
d	Trust in God (v. 3)	I trust in [God] (v. 27)	Repetition
e	[God] supports those who trust him in their trials, and their troubles, and their afflictions (v. 3)	[God] supported me in my trials, and troubles of every kind, yea, and in all manner of afflictions (v. 27)	Repetition
f	[I] shall be lifted up at the last day (v. 3)	[God] will raise me up at the last day (v. 28)	Repetition
g	I know of myself ... not of the carnal mind but of God (v. 4)	As I do know; and the knowledge which I have is of God (v. 26)	Repetition
h	[I am] born of God (v. 5)	Many have been born of God (v. 26)	Repetition

No.	Point	Counterpoint	Type
i	For I went about with the sons of Mosiah, seeking to destroy the church of God (v. 6)	Yea, and from that time even until now, I have labored without ceasing, that I might bring souls unto repentance; that I might bring them to taste of the exceeding joy of which I did taste; that they might also be born of God, and be filled with the Holy Ghost (v. 24)	Reversal
j	I fell to the earth; and it was for the space of three days and three nights that I could not open my mouth, neither had I the use of my limbs (v. 10)	[After three days and nights] my limbs did receive their strength again, and stood upon my feet (v. 23)	Reversal

No.	Point	Counterpoint	Type
k	The very thoughts of coming into the presence of my God did rack my soul with inexpressible horror. Oh, thought I, that I could be banished and become extinct both soul and body, that I might not be brought to stand in the presence of my God, to be judged of my deeds. (v. 14-15)	[After being forgiven,] my soul did long to be [in God's presence] (v. 22)	Reversal
l	I was thus racked with torment (v. 17)	I could remember my pains no more (v. 19)	Reversal
m	I was harrowed up by the memory of my many sins (v. 17)	I was harrowed up by the memory of my sins no more (v. 19)	Reversal
n	Jesus Christ, a Son of God (v. 17)	O Jesus, thou Son of God (v. 18)	Repetition

The pattern Alma designed was Repetition → (8×) → Reversal → (5×) → Repetition.

And visualizing the concept pairs within each theme shows the deliberate creation of the internal structure:

Part 2: Alma 36's Multifaceted Structure   207

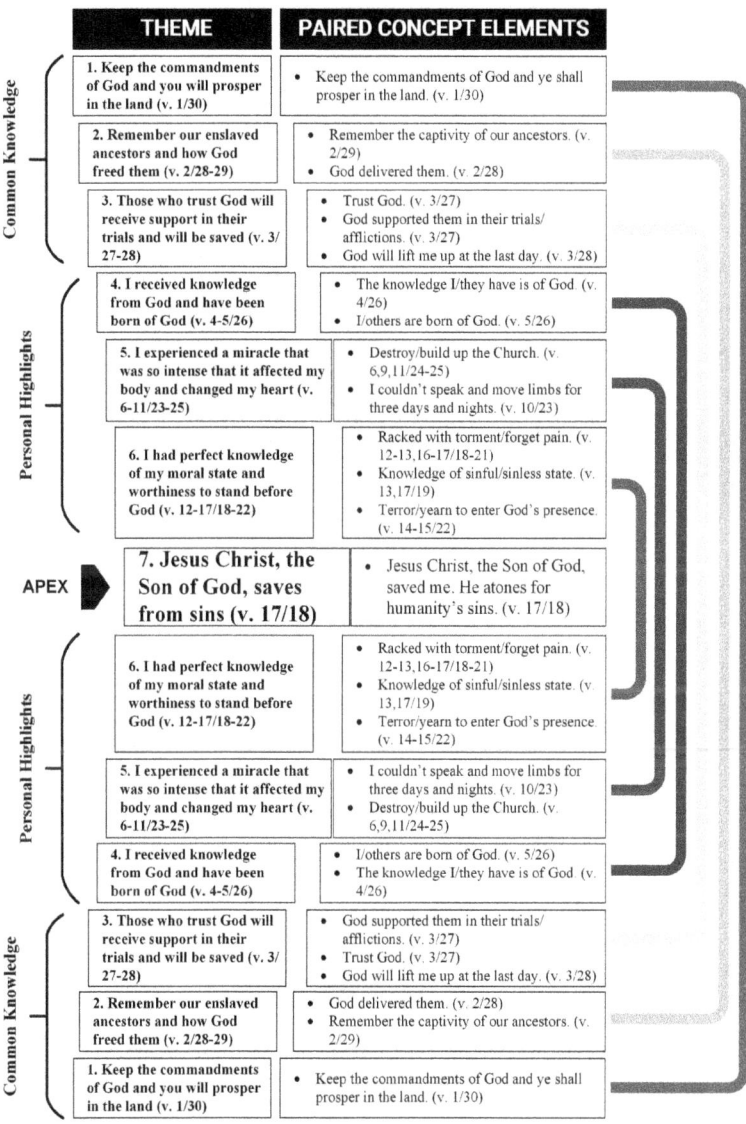

Figure 19: *Alma 36's Chiastic Structure With Paired Unsequenced Concept Elements*

Figure 19 shows Alma 36 is objectively a thematic chiasm with paired concept elements. It is unnecessary for the paired concept elements to be a chiasmus within their themes (hence the bullets, since their sequence is irrelevant), only that they are _present_ within the paired themes – which _are_ in a chiastic structure. There is no confirmation bias since the paired concepts are within their proper theme. The seven-element thematic chiasm structure covers every word within the chapter, both inside and outside the paired concept elements.

Furthermore, note that it is possible to create _three_ chiasmus structures at the same time within Alma 36:

1. Category-level: Common Knowledge-Personal Highlights-*Apex*-Personal Highlights-Common Knowledge
2. Theme-level: 1-2-3-4-5-6-7-6-5-4-3-2-1
3. Concept Element level: [a]-[b,c]-[d,e,f]-[g,h]-[i,j]-[k,l,m]-*[n]*-*[n]*-[k,l,m]-[i,j]-[g,h]-[d,e,f]-[b,c]-[a]

What explains this intricate complexity?

How Alma Created the Thematic chiasm

Creating a thematic chiasm requires thought and planning – one needs to think about what to write and where to place it. Then, paired words and concepts must be emplaced within the correct themes and integrated into an overall narrative.

Part 2: Alma 36's Multifaceted Structure

This multi-step process is easier said than done.

Fortunately, we can reconstruct how Alma created the thematic chiasm since the process is identical to making such a structure today.

Step 1: Create a thematic outline in chiasmus form.

The first thing Alma did was write down the outline of what he wanted his speech to say to a mostly illiterate audience who absorbed knowledge from oral discourse. The outline was the topic sections that made up the speech.

1. Keep the commandments of God, and you will prosper in the land

2. Remember our enslaved ancestors and how God freed them

3. Those who trust God will receive support in their trials and will be saved

4. I received knowledge from God and have been born of God

5. I experienced a miracle that was so intense that it affected my body and changed my heart

6. I had perfect knowledge of my moral state and worthiness to stand before God

7. Jesus Christ, the Son of God, atones for humanity's sins

> 6. I had perfect knowledge of my moral state and worthiness to stand before God
>
> 5. I experienced a miracle that was so intense that it affected my body and changed my heart
>
> 4. I received knowledge from God and have been born of God
>
> 3. Those who trust God will receive support in their trials and will be saved
>
> 2. Remember our enslaved ancestors and how God freed them
>
> 1. Keep the commandments of God, and you will prosper in the land

All the audience needed to do was remember the seven themes—three of which they already knew.

Step 2: Create paired words and concepts and place them within the paralleled themes.

After Alma created the outline, he inserted 1-3 subitems within each topic block that speak to the section in an organized way. These could be words, phrases, or ideas that will be fleshed out afterward.[28]

---

[28] To illustrate this another way, imagine using a word processing software. The Heading 1 of a new document is the thematic outline, and the Heading 2s are the subitems of the topic block. When the

1. Keep the commandments of God, and you will prosper in the land.

  a. Keep the commandments of God, and ye shall prosper in the land.

2. Remember our enslaved ancestors and how God freed them.

  b. Remember the captivity of our ancestors.

  c. God delivered our ancestors.

3. Those who trust God will receive support in their trials and will be saved.

  d. Trust God.

  e. God supports those who trust him in their trials and afflictions.

  f. God will lift up those who trust him on the last day.

4. I received knowledge from God and have been born of God.

  g. The knowledge I have is of God.

  h. I am born of God.

5. I experienced a miracle that was so intense that it affected my body and changed my heart.

---

table of contents is generated, the two tiers become visible on a single page.

i. My attitude toward the Church.

  j. I could not speak and move my limbs for three days and nights.

  6. I had perfect knowledge of my moral state and worthiness to stand before God.

  k. The awareness of my sins.

  l. The awareness of my salvific state.

  m. My feelings at entering God's presence.

  7. Jesus Christ, the Son of God, atones for humanity's sins.

  n. Jesus Christ is the Son of God who atones for humanity's sins.

  6. I had perfect knowledge of my moral state and worthiness to stand before God.

  k. The awareness of my sins.

  l. The awareness of my salvific state.

  m. My feelings at entering God's presence.

  5. I experienced a miracle that was so intense that it affected my body and changed my heart.

  i. My attitude toward the Church.

  j. I could not speak and move my limbs for three days and nights.

4. *I received knowledge from God and have been born of God.*

    g. The knowledge I have is of God.

    h. Others are born of God.

3. *Those who trust God will receive support in their trials and will be saved.*

    d. Trust God.

    e. God supports those who trust him in their trials and afflictions.

    f. God will lift up those who trust him on the last day.

2. *Remember our enslaved ancestors and how God freed them.*

    b. Remember the captivity of our ancestors.

    c. God delivered our ancestors.

1. *Keep the commandments of God, and you will prosper in the land.*

    a. Keep the commandments of God, and ye shall prosper in the land.

Step 3: Integrate the paired words and concepts with the surrounding text.

After Alma finished identifying the components of each topic, he then fleshed out each block. The words and phrases he wanted to be paired were then placed within the paired themes, and the concepts were expressed either using the same phrases (repetition), by their counterpart (reversal), or by their parallel (partner). The unpaired elements were written to support the paired elements while filling out the thoughts for clarity and content.

For example (in v. 1-5): My brethren/son, give ear to my words; for I swear unto you, that inasmuch as ye shall *keep the commandments of God ye shall prosper in the land.*

I would that ye should do as I have done, in *remembering the captivity of our fathers*; for they were in bondage, and *none could deliver them except it was the God of Abraham, and the God of Isaac, and the God of Jacob; and he surely did deliver them* in their afflictions.

And now, O my brethren/son, I beseech of thee that thou wilt hear my words and learn of me; for I do know that whosoever shall put their *trust in God shall be supported in their trials, and their troubles, and their afflictions,* and *shall be lifted up at the last day.*

And I would not that ye think that *I know of myself—not of the temporal but of the spiritual, not of the carnal mind but of God.*

Now, behold, I say unto you, if I had not been *born of God, I should not have known these things; but God has, by the mouth of his holy angel, made these things known unto me,* not of any worthiness of myself.

As can be seen, the text clearly shows such an organized approach.

Step 4: Revise, revise, revise.

To be effective, every speech, every study, and every essay needs revision after the initial draft. A persuasive essay is no different – it requires a "big picture" to kick it off – what does the author want to tell a specific audience? This results in creating an outline that can be comprised of just one tier or many tiers with multiple sublevels.

The writer then goes deep and starts writing one-dimensionally for the lowest subsection – letter by letter, until the particular thoughts are detailed. When all subsections are done, the author steps back and examines the text to see whether the pieces make sense relative to the whole. The author then changes the text, adds, deletes, and moves as needed. An editor may be employed to give it the touch required to be credible.

Alma clearly revised his speech for maximum impact on his audience. That's the only credible explanation for why Alma 36 has such an effective, organized structure.

Subsection Summary

The systematized nature of Alma 36 and the ease of its flow from thought to thought shows it is likely a refined persuasive public speech that has undergone many revisions where lessons learned were used to make it more effective to Alma's audience.

> *Thematic chiasm is the only chiastic model for Alma 36 that is immune to the confirmation bias or cherry-picking accusation since it encompasses every word of the chapter.*

Somehow, a seven-element thematic chiasm exists that contains over a dozen matching concept pairs in a symmetrical order that pivots on a central point: **Jesus Christ is the Son of God who atones for humanity's sins.** The thematic chiasm has common knowledge themes that sandwich Alma's personal highlights that he wants to use to convert people to Christ.

Part 2: Conclusion

This paper has demonstrated that Alma 36 is a persuasive essay tailored to an audience with a worldview that accepts as fact that God delivered their ancestors from captivity.

Merely changing one word six times and deleting nine words in a sentence is all that is needed to modify Alma 36 to a public speech version. Its structure is credible evidence that Alma 36 was probably a persuasive public speech of Alma's conversion story. This would have been Alma's most useful tool in bringing people to Christ, and it does not make sense for him not to capitalize on the public likely desire (to know more about the appearance of the angel that disrupted their lives).

Being a public speech explains why it contains a chiasmus – to aid the speaker in giving an organized address while helping the audience retain information. Its chiasmus comprises of seven themes that pivot on Jesus as the Son of God who atones for humanity's sins.

Everything about Alma 36 shows careful thought and attention to detail that results in a multi-dimensional coherent structure.

Creating a convincing persuasive essay is already very difficult to do, but to craft it in such a way that it also is a seven-element thematic chiasm with fourteen concept pairs is a skillset vastly higher than what can be expected outside a world-class university's writing lab.

These three facts of Alma 36 point to deliberate design in a manner that objectively cannot be dictated in a few hours. This begs the question:

How could Joseph Smith in 1829 dictate Alma 36 in just a few hours while he was looking at his seer stone?

He could either be a true prophet of God or the smartest person who ever lived. There are no other credible options given the objective evidence of Alma 36's deliberate design.

CONCLUSION

This book has shown that proof of deliberate design exists in the Book of Mormon despite being dictated – an empirical impossibility.

We know Joseph Smith dictated the book while looking at his seer stone, but the text itself does not show any evidence that it was produced in this manner. Instead, it shows the opposite: a complexity that can only be done by iterative writing.

What accounts for this discrepancy?

The Book of Mormon's internal organized complexity has always bothered skeptics who realize it could not have been dictated. They point to earlier works like View of the Hebrews[1] and Manuscript Found[2] as the source of the book. But none of these alleged sources contain the structured essay styles that comprise 34.1% of the Book of Mormon. And neither does it account for the twelve eyewitnesses to the dictation process.

Skeptics face an irreconcilable contradiction. The Book of Mormon objectively exists, and its contents clearly

---

[1] See https://archive.org/details/viewofhebrewsexh00smitrich to download a copy to compare the two.

[2] See https://archive.org/details/themanuscriptsto00spauuoft to download a copy to compare the two.

come from an iterative writing process. But the method used to transmit the structured text can never produce that type of literature, just like finding a book on the moon is an impossible process for book creation. So how did Joseph Smith do the impossible in 1829 if he was not a true prophet of God?

The outlier Book of Mormon claims it was written so that the world may believe that Jesus is the Christ, the Eternal God. Unless skeptics can replicate Joseph Smith's dictation process to produce structured literature like coherent argumentative essays, the Book of Mormon's claims must be taken seriously.

Take the 1200-Word Alma 36 Dictation Challenge

Experience is the best teacher, and it is always better to try something than keep it within the realm of theoretical when the benefits outweigh the risks.

And in the case of proving deliberate design in a known dictated book, the benefits are enormous: Verifiable evidence of the supernatural that validates the Christian faith, likely identification of the True Church out of over 30,000 candidates, and recognition within one's bones that Joseph Smith was a true prophet of God for doing something that you know from experience cannot be done.

A path in life suddenly gets illuminated that not only provides intellectual satisfaction but, most importantly, allows you to live a life of meaning and contentment, where you learn to love God, love your neighbor, love yourself, and keep God's commandments.

The Alma 36 challenge only requires two people, where you dictate ideas off the top of your head to someone who will write them down. It should last no more than two hours, which is more than the length of time Joseph Smith needed to dictate 1200 words.

Your challenge is to imitate Joseph Smith's creation of the tiny Alma 36 essay with its three facets following his dictation process.

Of course, you cannot replicate all the circumstances of the translation process since he was only a 23-year-old farmer with a third-grade education who lacked access to libraries and instructional material. There was no internet back in 1829, nor computers, electric lighting, and books that detail how to create argumentative essays and thematic chiasm.

You also have additional advantages that he did not have. Thanks to this book:

- You now know what an argumentative essay looks like. This helps you to create one intentionally.

- You now know what a thematic outline looks like.

- You know in advance that you are expected to create a public speech that will be customized for an individual.

We cannot change your advantages over Joseph Smith but will just have to work with it. But even then, there is no need for a handicap since the process itself is challenging enough.

Here are the conditions:

1. You cannot make any stylistic or structural change after the words leave your mouth. What your scribe writes down cannot be modified. After all, Alma 36 survives in the Original Manuscript in the same form we see today.
2. You have two hours to get it done.
3. No computer or internet to help you.
4. Your 1200-word essay must do three things at once:

   a. Be a coherent persuasive essay using an expository content style.

   b. Be a personalized public speech.

   c. Employ a thematic chiastic model of seven themes and fourteen paired concept elements.

That's it! So, grab your wife or buddy, promise them dinner if they are willing to act as your scribe for two hours, give them a pen and some paper, and have them sit at a table while you start dictating while staring at a stone.

Think of a topic,[1] come up with a thesis statement, craft several arguments that support the thesis, and provide multiple pieces of evidence for each argument. Do not forget to create a conclusion that restates your thesis, issues a call to action, and attempts to modify the audience's worldview.

While you are trying to keep all of that in your head, ensure that the essay is a modified public speech and especially make sure that it is a thematic chiasm with fourteen paired concept elements.

So, please try it and examine the results afterward. You will quickly realize that you cannot do it. Although you possess vast advantages over Joseph Smith, you will not be able to duplicate Alma 36's complexity using the same dictation process, especially when using the "first draft is the final draft" methodology.

---

[1] Some examples of topics that are worth exploring are: "NBA basketball" with a "Michael Jordan is the greatest basketball player of all time" thesis statement; "food" with a "Bacon is the greatest meal partner" thesis statement; "nation-state" with a "The USA is the greatest nation in history" thesis statement.

Conducting this exercise drives home the impossibility of Joseph Smith's accomplishment. When one attempts to imitate his translation process, even the most skilled and educated person faces an overwhelming sense of inadequacy because our brains are not wired to dictate structured essays.

It does not matter what you think about him—a true prophet of God or an immoral con man—he did something that none of us can do: dictate highly complex structured essays like Alma 36.

What explains this empirical impossibility in a book that claims it was written to convince the world that "Jesus is the Christ, the Eternal God"?

POSTSCRIPT: JOSEPH SMITH'S SEER STONE AND INTERPRETERS

While off-topic to the core contents of this book, this subject provides a fascinating context to the Book of Mormon's creation.

Figure 20: Joseph Smith's Seer Stone [1]

Eyewitness accounts describe Joseph Smith using his seer stone to dictate the Book of Mormon to his scribes. He would put the stone in a hat and even put his face into

---

[1] Photograph by Welden C. Andersen and Richard E. Turley Jr. (Church History Library, Salt Lake City). https://www.joseph smithpapers.org/topic/seer-stone. © By Intellectual Reserve, Inc. Used with permission.

it to block out outside light to see the words that appeared.²

At the same time, Smith claimed he used the interpreters that came with the Gold Plates when he finally obtained them on September 22, 1827. The interpreters were "two stones in silver bows—and these stones, fastened to a breastplate."³ The "spectacle" assembly could be detached and placed in a pouch at the front of the breastplate.

Figure 21: Artist Concept of the Interpreters⁴

---

² https://www.churchofjesuschrist.org/study/history/topics/book-of-mormon-translation?lang=eng; https://www.churchofjesuschrist.org/study/history/topics/seer-stones?lang=eng

³ Joseph Smith—History 1:35.

⁴ Replica and photograph by Jeneffer M. Watson. All rights reserved.

Joseph Smith started the translation process by wearing the breastplate and looking at the Gold Plates through the interpreters to read the English text. He later just used the detachable spectacle portion for convenience, and he no longer needed to look at the text on the Gold Plates to get their English equivalent. This was when he started putting the interpreters in a hat and covering up the Gold Plates.

At some point, he stopped using the interpreters and switched over to his seer stone. No reason was ever given for the change, but it is possible to make assumptions (see below). Both the interpreters and the seer stone were later referred to as the "Urim and Thummim," making it difficult to tell which was which.

The interpreters were directly used when Emma Smith and her brother, Reuben Hale, acted as Smith's scribes from December 1827 to April 1828. They were still in use when Martin Harris became the scribe on April 12, 1828:

The two stones set in a bow of silver were about two inches in diameter, perfectly round, and about five-eighths of an inch thick at the centre; but not so thick at the edges where they came into the bow. They were joined by a round bar of silver, about three-eighths of an inch in diameter, and about four inches long, which, with the two stones, would make eight inches.

> *The stones were white, like polished marble, with a few gray streaks. I never dared to look into them by placing them in the hat, because Moses said that "no man could see God and live," and we could see anything we wished by looking into them; and I could not keep the desire to see God out of my mind. And beside, we had a command to let no man look into them, except by the command of God, lest he should "look aught and perish."*[5]

The transition to exclusively using the seer stone likely happened either during Martin Harris's term as a scribe or after the loss of the 116 pages (where Harris lost all the transcriptions he did as well as all the work that Emma and Reuben did before him).

There is little doubt that Smith used the seer stone instead of the interpreters to dictate the entire Book of Mormon that we have today. But what is also true is that **the interpreters were *near* Smith and the Gold Plates while the dictation process occurred**. The interpreters and Gold Plates were always together—the angel gave them to Smith as a package, took them away together due to the 116-page fiasco, returned them as a pair, and then retrieved them together after the Book of Mormon was finished.

---

[5] Nicholson, R. p. 130. "Martin Harris Interview with Joel Tiffany, 1859," in Early Mormon Documents, 2:305.

This raises numerous questions.

1. Why did Joseph Smith stop using the interpreters and switch to the seer stone if the interpreters could do the job?

2. What advantages did the seer stone possess that were missing with the interpreters?

3. What risks did the interpreters pose that were absent with the seer stone?

4. Why were the interpreters always with the Gold Plates?

5. Why did Joseph Smith discard the seer stone and give it to Oliver Cowdery when they finished the Book of Mormon?

The interpreters were very powerful—terrifyingly so. The temptation to misuse them—a fatal punishment—would have been overwhelming to Smith since he would be able to see *whatever* he wanted (see Mosiah 8:13 cf. D&C 130:7-8), including things that could alleviate his family's poverty. He could find out where buried treasure was located. He could see Christ's crucifixion and resurrection. He could observe what the US president would be doing in the Oval Office a hundred years in the future.

We humans are not mature enough to use a tool that shows us whatever we want to see, no matter when or where.

Smith's switch to the seer stone removed the risk of misusing the interpreters. He must have breathed a sigh of relief, knowing that he could continue the translation process using a tool that he could not abuse to satisfy his curiosity or enrich himself.

The change raises another question: How did the seer stone make the process safer if the interpreters were still present and always with the Gold Plates?

This means the mechanics of the change were:

a. A dampening of the power of the interpreters (just like clip-on sunglasses reduces the sun's intensity on the eyes even though the eyeglasses itself is the thing responsible for helping the person see), or

b. A process conversion, where the interpreters functioned as a broadcaster that was transmitting the Book of Mormon text, and the seer stone was a receiver "tuned" to that frequency (comparable to how radios work), or

c. A redirection, where the interpreters functioned as a broadcaster and the seer stone was a relay that was synchronized to the same frequency (station to communication relay).

All options create a physical distance between Smith and the interpreters to reduce the temptation to misuse them. All options also harmonize what the eyewitnesses saw (Smith used the seer stone) with what Smith claimed (he used the interpreters). Both are correct:

a1. The eyewitnesses saw the polarized lens above the eyeglasses while Smith was talking about the eyeglasses itself.

b1. The eyewitnesses saw the radio while Smith was talking about the radio station.

c1. The eyewitnesses saw the relay switch while Smith was referring to the station.

In other words, the Book of Mormon was translated "by the gift and power of God" using the interpreters, but the seer stone was the tool that made the process safe for Joseph Smith and others. It possessed all the interpreters' advantages for translating the Book of Mormon without risking death from misusing it.

The seer stone became useless after the angel retrieved the Gold Plates and interpreters, which explains why Smith gifted it to Cowdery when they were done. It became nothing more than a paperweight.

The much-maligned and oft-ridiculed Joseph Smith did something we know is impossible. What explains the dictated Book of Mormon other than proof that *"Jesus is the Christ, the Eternal God"*?

BIBLIOGRAPHY

Barrett, D. B., Kurian, G. T., and Johnson, T. M. (2001). *World Christian Encyclopedia*. Oxford University Press.

Black, S. and Skinner, A. [eds.] (2005). *Joseph: Exploring the Life and Ministry of the Prophet*. Deseret Books.

Book of Mormon Translation. (n.d.). Www.churchofjesuschrist.org. Retrieved April 19, 2022, from https://www.churchofjesuschrist.org/study/history/topics/book-of-mormon-translation?lang=eng

Brown, S. K. (1992). *Alma's Conversion: Reminiscences in His Sermons. In Alma, the Testimony of the Word*. Charles D. Tate, Monte S. Nyman Deseret Book Company. [Behind paywall; accessed: 2020-04-18] http://www.gospelink.com/library/document/19763. n.d.

Chiasmus Index | Chiasmus Resources. Chiasmusresources.org, chiasmusresources.org/chiasmus-index. Accessed 23 Aug. 2022.

Christensen, C. M., Allworth, J., Dillon, K. (2012). *How Will You Measure Your Life?* Harper Business.

Covey, S. R. (1989). *The 7 Habits of Highly Effective People: Restoring the Character Ethic*. Fireside.

Edwards, Boyd F., Edwards W. F. (2004). *Does Chiasmus Appear in the Book of Mormon by Chance?* BYU Studies 43, no. 2.

FAIR. Chiasmus in the Book of Mormon: *What is special about the chiasmus found in Alma 36?* Retrieved February 2, 2022, from https://www.fairmormon.org/answers/Book_of_Mormon/Evidences/Hebraisms/Chiasmus, n.d.

Frankl, V. E. (1959, 1962, 1984). *Man's Search for Meaning: An Introduction to Logotherapy.* Third Edition. Touchstone Books.

Maxwell, N. A. (1997). *By the Gift and Power of God.* Ensign Magazine.

Newman, S. P. (1827). *A Practical System of Rhetoric: Or, the Principles and Rules of Style, Inferred from Examples of Writing.* New York: Mark H. Newman. Retrieved February 2, 2022, from https://archive.org/details/practicalsystemo00newmuoft.

Nicholson, R. (2013) *The Spectacles, the Stone, the Hat, and the Book: A Twenty-first Century Believer's View of the Book of Mormon Translation.* Interpreter: A Journal of Mormon Scripture, Volume 5 (2013), pp. 121-190.

Reynolds, N. B. (2018). *Rethinking Alma 36.* BYU ScholarsArchive, All Faculty Publications. 2104.

Seer stone – Glossary Topic. (n.d.). Www.josephsmithpapers.org. Retrieved April 19, 2022, from https://www.josephsmithpapers.org/topic/seer-stone

Seer Stones. (n.d.). Www.churchofjesuschrist.org. Retrieved April 19, 2022, from https://www.churchofjesuschrist.org/study/history/topics/seer-stones?lang=eng

Skousen, R. (1997). Book of Mormon Authorship Revisited: The Evidence for Ancient Origins. criticaltext.byustudies.byu.edu/translating-book-mormon-evidence-original-manuscript. Accessed 26 Aug. 2022.

— (2001). *The Original Manuscript of the Book of Mormon*. The Foundation for Ancient Research and Mormon Studies.

Skousen, R. [Ed.] (2009). *The Book of Mormon: The Earliest Text*. Yale University Press.

Skousen, R. and Jensen, R. (2015). *The Joseph Smith Papers. Revelations and Translations, Volume 3, Part 1 Printer's Manuscript of The Book of Mormon, 1 Nephi 1-Alma 35*. The Church Historian's Press.

Toulmin, S. (2003). *The Uses of Argument* (2nd ed.). Cambridge: Cambridge University Press. doi:10.1017/CBO9780511840005

Welch, J. W. (1970). *Chiasmus in the Book of Mormon*. BYU Studies Quarterly, Vol 10: Issue 1, Article 10.

— *(1991). A Masterpiece: Alma 36. Rediscovering the Book of Mormon.* FARMS.

— *(2007). The Discovery of Chiasmus in the Book of Mormon: Forty Years Later.* Journal of Book of Mormon Studies 16/2.

— (2018) *Timing the Translation of the Book of Mormon.* BYU Studies Quarterly. Vol 57, No. 4.

Wunderli, E. M. (2005) *Critique of Alma 36 as an Extended Chiasm.* Dialog: A Journal of Mormon Thought 38. no. 4.

Wurmbrand, R. (1967, 1998, 2013). *Tortured For Christ.* Living Sacrifice Book Company.

INDEX

21% of the Book of Mormon are argumentative and persuasive essays..... 16, 105

34.1% of the Book of Mormon are structured essays...... 22, 105, 219

Alma 36 challenge .. 11, 29, 221

Alma's conversion story .. 183, 216

Argument Type
  Abduction .. 36, 38, 40, 56, 57, 61, 69, 70, 84, 94, 158, 163
  Argument from Analogy ... 66, 94
  Deduction .. 33, 34, 35, 51, 52, 53, 57, 59, 65, 66, 67, 77, 79, 80, 84, 85, 86, 88, 94, 158, 161, 162, 163, 164
  Induction ... 35, 37, 39, 41, 43, 44, 52, 53, 54, 58, 60, 68, 69, 70, 78, 79, 80, 82, 94, 159, 160

Argument/evidence pairing 8, 15, 17, 90, 107, 113, 153

Argumentation-Contemporary Prophetic essay 27

Argumentation-Expository essay 27, 78

Argumentation-Missionary essay 27, 47, 64

Argumentative essay
  Three-dimensional structure 3, 8

Argumentative Essay
  Analytical tools 9

Argumentative essay structure 10, 113

Argumentative essays 8, 9, 15, 16, 18, 24, 28, 29, 30, 92, 93, 220, 221

Belief and knowledge
  Differences of 51

Book of Mormon
  28% of Original Manuscript still exists 5, 110
  Dictated first draft is the final draft 6, 29, 93, 110, 223
  Dictation creation process ... 3, 5, 7, 9, 15
  Evidence for God 2, 12
  Nearly 100% of Printer's Manuscript still exists 5
  No structural changes after dictation 5
  Not a creative writing book 6
  Overall structure is narrative 7

237

Proof of deliberate design 3, 8, 10

Utilitarian 6

Book of Mormon creation process

Eyewitnesses to the . 8, 15, 28, 33, 54, 151, 219, 231

Book of Mormon people's worldview 19

Born of God 158, 159, 161, 162, 163, 164, 171, 172, 177, 189, 191, 192, 196, 197, 204, 205, 209, 210, 211, 213, 214

Brass Plates 19, 78

Chiasmus 11, 147, 148, 151, 152, 180, 181, 182, 183, 186, 187, 192, 193, 208, 209, 216, 217

Conclusion of an argumentative essay .. 8, 15, 107, 113

Confirmation bias 30, 182, 193, 208, 216

Content Style
  Contemporary prophetic 26
  Expository 26, 156
  Parental 156
  Remote prophetic 26

Content styles.... 10, 22, 25, 26, 93, 156

Counterarguments
  Required for an argumentative essay 21, 23, 62, 71, 91, 94, 95, 107, 108, 119, 153, 154

Cultural baseline 169, 187, 188

David Whitmer 28

Deliberate design.... 3, 8, 9, 10, 25, 28, 47, 147, 151, 217, 219, 220

Descriptive Essay 24, 156

Dictation
  Characteristics of 3, 8

Dictation process 3, 4, 8, 12, 15, 93, 107, 111, 151, 219, 220, 223

Documentation analysis tools 115, 131

Dross 63, 91

Emma Smith 15, 28, 227

Empirical study benchmark 108, 110, 111, 112, 114, 130, 131, 142

English department
  Has tools to analyze documents 9

Essays
  Require an iterative process . 3

Evidence Type
  Objective ... 33, 34, 35, 51, 52, 53, 54, 57, 58, 59, 65, 66, 67, 77, 78, 79, 80, 84, 85, 88, 158, 161, 163, 164
  Subjective .. 35, 36, 37, 38, 39, 40, 41, 43, 44, 52, 53, 56,

57, 60, 61, 66, 68, 69, 77, 80, 82, 86, 158, 159, 160, 162, 163

Evidence-based practice....106

Exposition Essay 156

Exposition-Authoritative essay
The most dominant of all essays 27

Expository Essay 24, 25

Go/No-Go gate 107, 118

Gold Plates.........226, 227, 228, 229, 230, 231

Gordian Knot Cutter 148

Gospel, The 73, 75

Hellenistic Period worldview 18

Infinite Atonement, The.....78, 79, 80, 82, 86, 89, 91

Infinity 40, 78, 79, 80, 81, 82, 86, 89, 91

Interpreters 4, 226, 227, 228, 229, 230, 231

Islamic Golden Age worldview 18

Jacob, the "theologian" 31

Jesus Christ's Atonement
Bi-directional.....................40

Jesus is the Christ, the Eternal God ...2, 4, 9, 12, 16, 30, 220, 224

John Whitmer 15

Joseph Smith.......3, 4, 5, 7, 8, 9, 11, 15, 28, 29, 46, 47, 64, 75, 93, 107, 109, 110, 111, 112, 113, 114, 119, 142, 147, 150, 151, 152, 217, 219, 220, 221, 222, 223, 224, 225, 226, 227, 229, 231

Known-known 1

Known-unknown...................1

Koran 18, 19

Legal brief
Example of an argumentative essay................... 15, 18, 28

Lehi's Dream 24, 25, 97

Linear regression 130, 142

Literary criticism tools 10

Literary theory
Critical theory 10, 154
Formalism-Structuralism hybrid........................2, 10
Marxist theory 10, 155
New Historicism 10, 154
Psychoanalytical theory 10, 155

Literary theory lenses.........10, 154

Martin Harris 28, 227, 228

Medieval Europe worldview 18

Memory retention technique
Forward and backward
passes 184, 193

Michael Morse 15, 28

Narrative essays 25

Nephi's Panoramic
Vision 24, 27, 97

Nephi's Prayer 24, 25

Objective impossibility 1, 2, 8, 9

Olive Tree Allegory 25

Oliver Cowdery 11, 15, 28, 108, 229, 231

Oral Torah 19

Oral transmission of
knowledge 183, 209

Original Manuscript 5, 11, 110, 150, 222

Paired concept elements .. 147, 148, 208, 222, 223

Patent application
Example of an argumentative essay 15, 18

Persuasion Strategy
Ethos ... 33, 34, 35, 44, 54, 63, 77, 78, 90, 95, 158
Kairos 82, 83, 84, 90, 95
Logos ... 35, 36, 37, 38, 39, 40, 41, 43, 51, 52, 53, 56, 57, 58, 59, 63, 65, 66, 67, 68, 77, 78, 79, 80, 90, 95, 158, 161, 162, 163, 164

Pathos 56, 60, 61, 63, 69, 70, 72, 82, 84, 85, 86, 88, 90, 95, 159, 160, 163

Persuasion-Contemporary
Prophetic essay 27

Persuasion-Expository
essay 27, 30

Persuasion-Missionary
essay 27

Persuasive essays ... 10, 11, 15, 16, 17, 18, 20, 21, 24, 28, 30, 46, 92, 93, 147, 150, 152, 153, 154, 165, 167, 179, 215, 216, 217, 222

Poetry 6, 17

Printer's Manuscript 5

Proposed empirical
study 106

Prose 6, 17

Qualitative documentation
analytics 2, 3
Concept development 3
Internal structure 2

Quantification of the
dictation process 107

Rabbinic Judaism
worldview 19

Reuben Hale 28, 227

Rhetorical Mode
Argumentation 156
Exposition 156
Persuasion 156

Index 241

Rhetorical Mode-Content Style classification 27

Rhetorical modes 10, 22, 23, 29, 93, 156

Richard Wurmbrand 41, 46

Rubric .. 107, 119, 130, 138, 142

Samuel Newman 29

Samuel the Lamanite 27, 103, 156

Scatterplot 130, 142

Scientific method 18

Scribal anticipation 5

Scribes of Joseph Smith 3, 5, 15, 109, 225, 227

Seer stone 4, 7, 15, 28, 109, 147, 151, 217, 219, 225, 227, 228, 229, 230, 231

South Park
   All About the Mormons episode 15

Statistical analysis 107, 115, 119, 130, 131

Stephen Toulmin 29

Structured essays
   One-third of the Book of Mormon are 7, 22

Subjective-Abductive argument 40

Subjective-Inductive argument 43

Thematic chiasm 11, 148, 150, 152, 183, 191, 208, 209, 216, 217, 221, 223

Thesis statement 8, 15, 16, 17, 18, 23, 24, 46, 76, 90, 107, 113, 153, 223

Torah 19

Toulmin model of argument 16

Unknown-unknown 1

Urim and Thummim 227

Viktor Frankl 41, 46

Warrant
   Needed to support a thesis statement 18, 24

Worldview
   Argumentative essay effectiveness depends on the audience's 1, 18, 19, 31, 37, 46, 48, 52, 65, 77, 78, 84, 88, 166, 167, 216, 223

ABOUT THE AUTHOR

Edward K. Watson has over 70,000 hours in writing, editing, and analyzing complex documents such as RFPs, proposals, and project execution plans for very large projects, including a dozen in the billion-dollar range. He is the author  of the four-volume *Is Jesus "God"? A Witness to the World That Jesus is the Christ, the Eternal God*. The work details the only empirical evidence that anyone can use to justify the belief that the Holy Bible is inspired by God (the New Testament is a frameless, unharmonized, correlative anthology). The book also provides three additional pieces of evidence that support belief in God and demolishes atheism.

He published his first book in 1998 (***Mormonism***), but lost interest in Latter-day Saint apologetics and discontinued the series. After a decade as an atheist, he is, once again, a devout member of the Church of Jesus Christ of Latter-day Saints and has enormous appreciation for the teachings in the Book of Mormon concerning our God, Jesus Christ, and of his infinite Atonement.

Ed is awestruck by the Prophet Joseph Smith, by what that uneducated farmer accomplished in a mere 15 years before his death in 1844 at just 38 years of age. Ed points out that it does not matter whether one thinks Joseph Smith was a true prophet of God or a con man – his stacked accomplishments in over a dozen areas show he was a genius without peer. People do themselves a disservice by dismissing this *supernova* without thought because his "fruits" are objective and empirical (such as the Book of Mormon containing dozens of coherent argumentative essays despite being dictated—a demonstrable impossibility as anyone who has had to write them in university can attest). If he was not a true prophet of God, then what was he since no one can do what he did in similar circumstances?

It only took thirty years, thousands of books, and tens of thousands of dollars, but Ed is finally starting to understand that what is truly important in life is not what he knows, but who he is as a person. He finally gets what the Savior said when he told us to:

- LOVE GOD
- LOVE YOUR NEIGHBOR
- LOVE YOURSELF
- KEEP THE COMMANDMENTS

To be truly wise and content means to live a life of meaning, where we genuinely love. We can then leave this world with joy, knowing that as God is, so are we (1 John 4:16-17).

www.ingramcontent.com/pod-product-compliance
Lightning Source LLC
Chambersburg PA
CBHW072224200426
43209CB00073B/1932/J